VARIETY OF WAYS

VARIETY OF WAYS

Discussions on Six Authors

By

BONAMY DOBRÉE

Essay Index Reprint Series

Originally published by:

OXFORD

AT THE CLARENDON PRESS

1932

BOOKS FOR LIBRARIES PRESS, INC.

FREEPORT, NEW YORK

First published 1932
Reprinted 1967

PRINTED IN THE UNITED STATES OF AMERICA

PREFACE

ONE of the reasons why we read, presumably, is to find out what other people are like; and one of the reasons why we make ourselves familiar with various authors, is to find out in what variety of ways they tackled living. The six authors here discussed (two from one work only) represent six quite distinct attitudes towards life. Dryden was concerned almost wholly with his art, with language; the rest of life, given reasonable comfort, was in the main indifferent to him. To Halifax the world was everything, the world in its best sense, with its responsibilities as well as its graces; whereas to Bunyan, this world was as nothing; his business was with the next. Congreve and Steele were more complicated. Congreve tried to dominate the crude chaos of life by stamping it with his own sensibility; Steele allowed himself to be utterly dominated by the chaos, in which he struggled in bewilderment, snatching what he could here and there. Mandeville is a kind of homespun, introspective Halifax—his epigram sometimes reminds us of Halifax; but his thought was based on quite a different kind of experience, the experience of the study or laboratory as opposed to that of the council and the Court. All lived at much the same time, in much the same world of ideas; but beyond that, and the fact that they could all write, there seems little enough to connect them.

Thus it would be idle to generalize, to draw a conclusion, to suggest a discovery, or to trace advance.

I only hope that this impossibility, as it seems to me, may itself prove fruitful. Without being (philosophically) an anarchist, you may feel that there are too many theories abroad; you jostle them on every pavement, or, rather, they jostle you. There is no one system that is best, no one way of life that is most meritorious. We sometimes feel that nowadays we are not to be allowed to sit quiet and look, especially not back upon old times to contemplate our forefathers: and this volume is an attempt to do so.

I will not for a moment pretend that my object in reading these men's works was to discover how they tackled life; I read their works because they pleased me, or taught me, or both. But the other issue emerges, unwittingly, when one begins to write about people: there is no end to the side-tracks of criticism, all called main roads by those who follow them, and some lead to the darkest pit of metaphysics, the mystico-metaphysical one. My object has been to evoke as coherent a figure as possible from the writings of each man; and by putting the figures together in one volume, I have aimed at giving each a value by contrast, which alone, perhaps, he would not have.

B. D.

CONTENTS

NOTE

THE chapters on Dryden, Halifax, and Steele originally appeared, much as they are here, in the *Times Literary Supplement*, the Editor of which has kindly allowed them to be reprinted here. The chapters on Bunyan and Congreve exist as Introductions in the World's Classics series: that on Mandeville was especially written for this book.

I
JOHN DRYDEN

D RYDEN had the great good luck to be born into
an age which did not try to fit art, or literature,
into some imagined scheme of values. In his day,
unless you were savagely Puritan, you accepted the
fact that literature had its proper place in life. There
was no question of its being a substitute for religion,
which was admitted to be a higher activity; nor did
it need to be based on some profound philosophy or
psychological theory, because these things were distinct. Naturally, letters were not to be used for evil
purposes: 'supposing verses are never so beautiful or
pleasing, yet if they contain anything which shocks
religion, or good manners, they are at best what
Horace says of good numbers without sense, *versus
inopes rerum, nugaeque canorae*,' Dryden wrote in the
Preface to the 'Fables'. On the other hand, poetry
might possibly do good in an indirect way:

By the harmony of words [the Preface to *Tyrannick Love*
tells us] we elevate the mind to a sense of devotion, as our
solemn music, which is inarticulate poesy, does in churches:
and by the lively images of piety, adorned by action, through
the senses allure the soul: which, while it is charmed in a
silent joy of what it sees and hears, is struck at the same time
with a secret veneration of things celestial, and is wound up
insensibly into the practice of that which it admires.

We need not, perhaps, take all this too seriously;
the little concern which Dryden showed for these
politic points is evidence enough that he did not need

B

to give them great attention. There was a realm of literature which existed on its own merits, and might be allowed to continue unhampered so long as it kept within certain large bounds. But if the bounds were large, they were definite; they marked off literature as a special province in which its own laws operated.

It was indeed admitted on all sides that poetry must instruct as well as delight, though what themes exactly it was to instruct in was left conveniently vague; and Dryden, with a grasp of implication denied to most of his contemporaries, was inclined to argue that the only way literature could instruct was by presenting existence in a manner more 'lively' than was to be met with in everyday experience: it could enlarge the domain of the passions. Shadwell, Rymer, Blackmore, and such like did, it is true, declare that art must depict the triumph of virtue, and that pleasure was a mere 'subordinate, subaltern end'; but Dryden was wiser. In his *Defence of an Essay of Dramatick Poesy* he remarked of it: 'I am satisfied if it cause delight: for delight is the chief, if not the only end of poesy; instruction can be admitted but in the second place, for poesy only instructs as it delights.' He is on the verge of saying that delight is itself instruction. However, what was important for him, for the work which he wanted to do, was that an atmosphere prevailed in which he could give himself wholly to the discussion of literary problems without being clogged with irrelevant issues: his mind could wander freely over the questions he loved to discuss and ponder; his steps were not trammelled with deeply mysterious consideration: in short, he could consider literature as a body of objects which, separately and as a whole, had certain definite characteristics.

The main problem, of course, was to discover what it was which gave delight; how it might best be produced; and sometimes, more rarely, trenching on the borders of psychology, to discover why pleasure was either born or blighted. It is on this last ground, for instance, that in the *Essay of Dramatick Poesy* Dryden defends the use of comic relief:

> Why should he [Lisideius] imagine the soul of man more heavy than his senses? Does not the eye pass from an un-pleasant object to a pleasant in a much shorter time than is needed to do this? . . . A continued gravity keeps the spirit too much bent; we must refresh it sometimes, as we bait in a journey, that we may go on with greater ease.

But he rarely touches on that aspect, for such things are taught by common sense; as far as general principles go, he is anxious to stress the difference between art and life, and in his controversy with Howard was careful to guard against the intrusion of realism. What was 'natural' in life was not 'natural' in plays. Howard accused him of mistaking the sense of the word natural, 'for 'tis not the question', he wrote, 'whether rhyme or not rhyme be the best and most natural for a grave and serious subject, but what is the nearest the nature of that which it presents'; to which Dryden answered: 'I wonder he should think me so ridiculous to dispute whether prose or verse be nearest to ordinary conversation.' The point was one of 'art, not of life—namely, whether verse 'be natural or not in plays'. And when

Howard submitted that a play was 'supposed to be
the composition of several persons speaking *ex tem-
pore*', Dryden retorted that on the contrary, a play
was 'supposed to be the work of a poet'. What was
the point of art if it was the same as life? Thus in
An Essay on Heroick Plays he declared roundly:

If any man object the improbabilities of a spirit appearing, or
of a palace raised by magic, I boldly answer him, that an
heroic poet is not tied to a bare representation of what is true,
or exceeding probable; but that he may let himself loose to
visionary objects, and to the representation of such things as
depending not on sense, and therefore not to be comprehended
by knowledge, may give him a freer scope for imagination.

The ground being thus cleared, he was at liberty to
turn to the considerations which really interested him;
and he moves with beautiful freedom in the realm of
technicalities. He is enchanting on the vexed question
of rhyme or blank verse in plays, on the roughness or
smoothness of verse, and even on what is apt to be, to
the layman, so tedious a subject as prosody. Thus in
the 'Dedication to Examen Poeticum':

Since I have named the *synalepha*, which is the cutting off
one vowel, immediately before another, I will give an example
of it from 'Chapman's Homer', which lies before me: for the
benefit of those that understand not the *Latine Prosodia*.
'Tis in the first line of the 'Argument to the first Iliad'.

Apollo's *Priest to th'*Argive *Fleet doth bring*, &c.

There we see he makes it not the *Argive*, but th'*Argive*, to
shun the shock of the two vowels, immediately following
each other; but in his second Argument, on the same page,
he gives a bad example of the quite contrary kind:

Alpha *the Pray'r of* Chryses *sings*:
The Army's Plague, the Strife of Kings.

In these words *the Army's, the* ending with a vowel, and *Army's* beginning with another vowel, without cutting off the first, by which it had been *th' Army's,* there remains a most horrible ill-sounding gap betwixt those words.

He is never pedantic, because he does not have to be. There is no mystery, because poetry is as much a part of everyday experience as anything else. He talks of literature as naturally and as interestingly as a mechanic will talk about an engine; if you do certain things, other things will happen; this portion works in this way because of that arrangement. There is no more need perpetually to discuss the ethics of literature than there is to argue the morality of engineering. Such considerations belong to a different department. Thus Dryden remains the purest and most inspiring example of the literary critic; and it is largely to that that he owes his outstanding position as the supreme English man of letters.

Not that Dryden as a critic stops short at the discussion of the purely mechanical side of verse—as though there could be a purely mechanical side; the way a man writes depends upon what a man is; not merely words alone, or thought applied to words, are his material, but his motive force is itself part of it, just as it is not the machine alone, but the fuel, which determines how the motor will run. And Dryden, bringing his highest critical powers to bear upon the authors he was to translate, under the sway (and indeed part author) of the theory that a translation should be what the Greek or Roman would write were he a living Englishman, held himself bound to appraise the character of his original poet before putting him into English. He is at his surest when discussing Lucretius in the Preface to *Sylvae*; not the thoughts of Lucretius, for with these as a literary critic he is not concerned, except to note what they were. Thus he lets fall in passing: 'As for his opinions concerning the mortality of the soul, they are so absurd, that I cannot, if I would, believe them.' What the poet might believe was not the point; what mattered was the nature of the man:

If I am not mistaken, the distinguishing character of Lucretius (I mean of his soul and genius) is a certain kind of noble pride, and positive assertion of his opinions. He is everywhere confident of his own reason, and assuming an absolute command, not only over his vulgar reader, but even his patron Memmius. . . .

And so the analysis goes on, an analysis which will at once describe the style, and give the reason for its being thus and not otherwise; he deduces the masculinity of the writing, the warmth of the argument, the 'scorn and indignation, as if he were assured of the triumph, before he entered into the lists'. Lucretius, he declares, might have been everywhere as poetic as in his descriptions, had he not been too eager to instruct: 'in short, he was so much an atheist, that he forgot sometimes to be a poet'. That, surely, is as far as criticism need go, or indeed can go. Pursue it further, and we enter other realms, more important, no doubt, to those who habitually dwell in them, but in which the criteria of literary criticism cease to apply.

Not that the poet was debarred from being didactic: that suggestion could not come from the

man who wrote the best instructive verse in the
language. He might have said of himself that he was
sometimes so much of a Christian that he could not
afford to be a poet: he did indeed say, at the end of
Religio Laici:

> And this unpolish'd rugged verse I chose,
> As fittest for discourse, and nearest prose;

but all that he meant was that he had denied himself
certain poetical fashions of the day. Heroic poetry
was not to be expected, he warned the reader in the
Preface; the poet might be majestic, but it was his
first business to be plain and natural:

> The florid, elevated and figurative way is for the passions;
> for love and hatred, fear and anger, are begotten in the soul
> by showing their objects out of their true proportion, either
> greater than the life or less; but instruction is to be given by
> showing them what they naturally are. A man is to be cheated
> into passion, but to be reasoned into truth.

The desire to teach, then, was no hindrance to the
poet, provided that he adapted his instrument; and
Dryden, in writing *Religio Laici* must have been well
aware that he was making poetry. Majesty at least is
not lacking:

> Dim as the borrow'd beams of moon and stars
> To lonely, weary, wand'ring travellers
> Is Reason to the soul: and as on high
> Those rolling fires discover but the sky,
> Not light us here; so Reason's glimmering ray
> Was lent, not to assure our doubtful way,
> But guide us upward to a better day.
> And as those nightly tapers disappear
> When day's bright lord ascends our hemisphere;

So pale grows Reason at Religion's sight;
So dies, and so dissolves in supernatural light.

Indeed, more than majesty is there, not in the simile
alone, which, no doubt, is commonplace enough
though brilliantly handled, but in the extraordinary
beauty of the versification, more especially in those
qualities which Miss Sitwell has taught us to call
texture. It demands no exquisite ear to detect the
magical vowel-modulations of the second line, its
achievement of what, to venture a barbarism, we
might call an 'emotional onomatopoeia', the very line
seeming to lag and falter with the fatigue of the
traveller. Read Dryden for the meaning alone and
you may well find him full of sturdy common sense
rather than of poetry; but to love him you must not
only listen to him but palate him on the tongue. Not
to do so would be to miss the amazingly deep caesura
after 'dissolves' in the last line quoted, a caesura
which gives the word which comes before it its full
emotional as well as intellectual meaning. Can we,
indeed, if we accept the argument of the poem, be
sure that we have not been cheated into truth rather
than reasoned into it? The manner, it is true, drops
a little, so that we may perhaps believe that it is
reason which guides us: but was it reason that wrote,
or is it reason that accepts and delights in the line
descriptive of God which follows so soon,

Unmade, unmoved; yet making, moving all?

If that is the verse nearest prose, let us have more
prosaic verse from our poets.

It is a famous, or at least a notorious, phrase of

Pater's that Dryden's fondness for distinguishing
prose from poetry came somewhat oddly from a man
whose own verse was so prosaic. But if Pater, himself so well able to make distinctions, had been less
blinded by the poetic fashions of his day, he might
have seen that this very 'prosaic' quality of Dryden's
verse was precisely that which enabled him to distinguish poetry from prose. Both, for him, were
instruments for the communication of thought and
feeling—not, Heaven forbid! for the expression of a
personality—instruments, moreover, which needed
to be hammered and forged into shape, to be refined
down and sharpened to the utmost. The chief work
of his long, patiently arduous life consisted in creat-
ing a language fit for civilized Englishmen to use;
that he should have done this was no mere accidental
result of his writings, but a task he undertook in full
consciousness of what he was doing. He saw, what
others at the same time were seeing, what had indeed
been seen before them, that English poetry, if it were
to develop, must recover some of the properties of
prose, properties which, if it had not altogether lost
them, it was at least in danger of losing, those
especially of clarity, directness of statement, im-
mediacy of effect and of nervous strength and supple-
ness. Poetry, however, is more concentrated than
prose, which, so we read in the preface to the *Fables*,
'allows more liberty of thought; and the expression
is more easy, when unconfined by numbers'. The
difference for Dryden was one not of kind but of
degree; poetry must be as nourishing as prose, not
like that of 'one of our late great poets . . . sunk in

reputation', because he provided 'whole pyramids of
sweetmeats for boys and women, but little solid meat
for men'. The other harmony of prose could be more
diffuse, even rambling. And if we read Dryden's
prose and Dryden's poetry with the smallest attention, we perceive that the difference—and surely it
is marked enough—consists as much in the greater
concentration of music as it does in the closer com-
pactness of thought. Lucid and concise as his prose
is, his poetry, especially when he is writing satire,
and hardly less so when he is didactic, is a miracle of
compression, and, besides, consummately musical.
But in his maturer verse the music is more dis-
ciplined than in his earlier; it is not so obvious as it is
in the *Annus Mirabilis*, where it may be found cloying:

> Methinks already, from this chymic flame,
> I see a city of more precious mold;
> Rich as the town which gives the Indies name,
> With silver paved, and all divine with gold.

Nobody can miss the tunefulness of that; it is of the
sort that gives Gray's *Elegy* its popularity. But to
forget the sense and catch the music of the description of Polyphemus shaving (in the fable of *Acis and
Galatea*) requires an ear more alert for the particular
qualities of Dryden's music:

> Assumed the softness of a lover's air,
> And comb'd, with teeth of rakes, his rugged hair.
> Now with a crooked scythe his beard he sleeks,
> And mows the stubborn stubble of his cheeks.

Unless it is claimed that subject, or emotional sensa-
tion, or the 'prophetic' tone alone constitute poetry,

those lines, with their discipline, their art, their order, may well serve as a norm from which all poetry diverges, sometimes to its benefit, as often to its cost.

Order, or the love of order, is perhaps the clue to Dryden's character, and may go far to explain, not only his passionate experiment in verse and in play-writing—and, for that matter, in the lyric—but also the change of his faith, to which some have ascribed only the most 'realistic' motives; a love of order which required and searched for some authority out-side the mere person, or mere taste, something to which private judgement must in the end conform. If *The Hind and Panther* was to express his conver-sion to Rome, and if *Religio Laici* contains hints that it was pending, the spring which was to move him is traceable in *The Medal*:

> The common cry is ev'n Religion's test;
> The Turk's is, at Constantinople, best;
> Idols in India; Popery at Rome;
> And our own worship only true at home.
> And there but for the time; 'tis hard to know
> How long we please it shall continue so.

The impulse there is clear enough; and we may be led to think that in all his work there is not only the love of order, visible in each verse, in the structure of every poem, and in the extraordinary grace of his plays, but also the desire to discover some absolute truth. He seems to search in Greek tragedy, in Shakespeare, in Corneille and Racine, not for knack, or tricks of the trade, as a man whom curiosity may move to 'find out the go of a thing'; but as a man eager to discover something which is true, not only

at home, or for the time, but everywhere and always,
something which will serve as a test and as authority;
and he seems to be glad when, in his bold experi-
mentation, he can find an oracle to support him.

But a love of order alone, even the power of
marshalling many things into order, is not enough
to explain Dryden, or indeed to make any author
readable. In the last resort the quality which tells
most, more than sensibility, more than intelligence,
is vigour. Dryden's sensibility is not exquisite;
where deep issues or philosophy are concerned, his
mind is humdrum; but vigour is there in abundance,
an energy which sparkles and delights, a directness
of purpose and means, a beautifully athletic motion
in all he does, and daring to attempt a surprising
variety of things. The vigour is really creative, for
seizing upon a subject, he does not leave it until he
has made an object out of it. As with Lucretius it
was the 'noble pride' as much as his subject which
formed the material of his poem, so with Dryden, the
man's own force seems to be part and parcel of the
thing he has made. As Coleridge wrote:

> The vividness of the descriptions or declamations in Donne
> or Dryden is as much and as often derived from the force and
> fervour of the describer, as from the reflections, forms or
> incidents, which constitute their subject and materials. The
> wheels take fire from the mere rapidity of their motion.

And Dryden, perhaps more than Donne, had control
of the motion; not always, indeed; since, in the
phraseology of his day, he sometimes allowed his
fancy, that 'high-ranging spaniel', to outrun his
judgement, especially in his earlier heroic plays; but

his prose is nearly impeccable. Landor, after speaking of his 'vigour, vivacity, and animation', goes on: 'He is always shrewd and penetrating, explicit and perspicuous, concise where conciseness is desirable, and copious where copiousness can yield delight.' The reference is to his poetry; but the phrases are at least as well applied to his prose.

It is no derogation of Dryden's mind to have said that on questions outside his art it was humdrum. Perhaps, however, it would be more just to say that he did not want to be bothered. As to religion, it may well have been scepticism together with a desire for authority that made him a Catholic:

> In seeking happiness you both agree;
> But in the search, the paths so different be
> That all religions with each other fight,
> While only one can lead us in the right.
> But till that one hath some more certain mark,
> Poor humane kind must wander in the dark.

Politics might almost be considered in the same way; there was no certainty, so one had better adhere to what was established. Thus he could, without loss of inner integrity, though with seeming inconsistency, write an ode to Cromwell, and welcome back the exiled King: and having once decided to remain loyal to the Stuarts, it would be almost too much trouble not to be a Jacobite. In the last thing he ever wrote, the astonishingly vigorous *Secular Masque*, he summed up the business pithily enough:

> All, all of a piece throughout;
> *To Diana.* Thy chase had a beast in view;
> *To Mars.* Thy wars brought nothing about;

To Venus.   Thy lovers were all untrue.
'Tis well an old age is out,
And time to begin a new.

Politics were good enough matter to serve for a brilliant satire, but in the main he wanted to be left alone to think about literature. No man can be great unless he gives himself wholly to one thing, and Dryden gave himself completely to letters. There, at least, he could be free from petty considerations:

For what other reason have I spent my life in so unprofit-able a study? [he asked in the 'Dedication to Examen Poeticum]: Why am I grown old in seeking so barren a reward as fame? The same parts and application, which have made me a poet, might have raised me to any honours of the gown, which are given to men of as little learning and less honesty than myself. No government has ever been, or ever can be, wherein time-servers and block-heads will not be uppermost. The persons are only changed, but the same jugglings in state, the same hypocrisy in religion, the same self-interest, and mismanagement, will remain for ever.

There had been squabbles in his life, faction, personal rivalries with hard hitting on both sides, but nothing could cloud the main issue. The work done was there, it could be seen and tested: in the world of letters, hypocrisy, self-interest, juggling, were no help in achieving fame: and certainly little else was to be got beyond a bare living. But, of course, what had really impelled Dryden to seek this mode of life was not a moral consideration, but love of the work: we feel, in the passage just quoted, that he knew he had done well, and that this knowledge was enough reward.

How well he had done his contemporaries could not see; it is only posterity which has been able to gauge his enormous influence on English and on style; and three-quarters of a century were to run before Johnson wrote 'he found the language brick and left it marble'. But what his contemporaries could and did see was the fact that he had produced writings in various departments of literature on the level of anything his fellow-writers produced, and that he had established almost a new form in satire. 'The new way of writing' verse or plays was a way in which he was only one of many artificers; but nobody else could sustain the rush of *Absalom and Achitophel*, or even of *Mac Flecknoe*; those would endure, for, like all great satirists, Dryden, like Jonson or Pope, created the object in destroying it. Shadwell and Shaftesbury may mean little or nothing to us now, but Mac Flecknoe and Achitophel are part of our consciousness of life. Yet whatever his contemporaries saw in him, they could not have seen what we do, for in the course of centuries materials sift themselves out; the confusion of a period clarifies at a distance; inessentials drop away. And what perhaps we now see is that Dryden was the master, above all who worked with or against him, of a particular kind of drama.

' 'Tis unjust,' he remarked in the Preface to *The State of Innocence*, 'that they who have not the least notion of heroic writing, should therefore condemn the pleasure which others receive from it, because they cannot comprehend it.' It is, no doubt, harder for us to comprehend it than it was for his contemporaries; but once we can detach it from life, once we can accept its artificiality, not as a blemish but as a virtue, we are in a fair way to enjoy it. It is a peculiar form, conditioned by the time, its essence being that it clothes the 'romantic' idea in 'classical' dress. Thus in Dryden's plays we must look for the grace, the charm, the 'turns of fancy'; we must delight in the structure, the movement, part dramatic part lyrical, even, as has been said, in the prettiness. Take this from *Aurengzebe*:

> Fortune long frowned, and has but lately smiled!
> I doubt a foe so newly reconciled.
> You saw but sorrow in its waning form,
> A working sea remaining from a storm;
> When the now weary waves roll o'er the deep,
> And faintly murmur ere they fall asleep.

That is not the language of life; nor is it that of great tragedy: but no one would wish to contend that 'an heroic poem' can stand up against the work of the Shakespearians (even if it can hold what is really its own); least of all did Dryden wish to do so. 'We trail our plays under them,' he declared: again and again he paid homage to Shakespeare: and we in our turn make a mistake if we judge Restoration tragedies in a class to which they were never meant to belong. Dryden said that he never felt quite at his ease in the drama; and indeed it is in narrative and satirical verse that he was more at home. But in the drama he constructed distinctive, solid objects, which it is rash to despise if we do not wish to lose an opportunity for delight: for in whatever he did we are always aware of the perfect handling of the instrument, of his care for language, and of the creative power of his word.

II

GEORGE SAVILE MARQUESS OF HALIFAX

IT is one of the graces of our history that so many of our statesmen have also been men of letters. It is as though that happy instinct which has guided us through so many trials had made us tend all unawares to the good government imagined by Plato—rule by good men, by men, that is, equipped with humane knowledge, endowed with the sense of values which only acquaintance with the thought of the ages can give. The tradition begins at least as early as Chaucer, and has lasted to our own day, dwindling now, it would seem, seeing that it is only in the ranks of our elder statesmen that these elect ones are to be found, and they are disappearing.

Not that George Savile, Marquess of Halifax, was a man of letters apart from his public life; it is because, like Bolingbroke, he stated his experience in the good prose of his age that he has his high place among authors. He did not invade the realms of philosophy or of imaginative writing, nor did he indulge in criticism or give himself to editorial labours. Half his writings at least are practical handbooks to the politics of his day; and it is a tribute to their depth and clarity of thought that they may be read with profit as well as with pleasure in ours. 'Any one who reads the pamphlets which contain Halifax's reflections on the controversies of his own time will find himself, almost against his will, applying these reflections to the matter of to-day,' Sir Walter Raleigh wrote; and though he prefaced the remark by saying, 'It is something to feel that we are not more fantastic or absurd than our ancestors,' he failed to note that, we do not, unless we are historians, so much as con over the pamphlets of other writers of the period, except those of Dryden, which survive not for their matter but for their rhyme. But then Savile has this quality of the great writer, that we scarcely know whether it be for his mind or for his style that·we read him; the latter follows the former so nearly that the words are not the clothing but the very spirit of his thought. We may say of him, as he said of Montaigne in his 'Letter to Charles Cotton': 'He scorned *affected Periods*, or to please the mistaken Reader with an empty *Chime* of *Words*. He hath no *Affectation* to set himself out, and dependeth wholly upon the *Natural Force* of what is his own.' Indeed, to set himself out would have been to labour in vain, for his pamphlets were all anonymous, and his most brilliant works, *Advice to a Daughter* and *The Character of Charles II*, were, like his Maxims, not meant for publication.

It is, we may say, his very qualities as a man of letters which prevent him from figuring large in school books of history, though on three separate occasions—the debate on the Exclusion Bill, the Declaration of Indulgence, and the Revolution—he was the pivot about which the fate of the nation turned; for these qualities are his refusal to go be-yond the point where his thought would lead him, and his aloofness from the factions and violence of

his day. It was precisely his fastidious integrity, his
aversion from setting himself out, which prevented
him from becoming a great leader. He could be
neither Danby on the one hand nor Shaftesbury on
the other—he was indeed instrumental in the fall of
both; and since it is the tumultuary opinion which
cries, 'Because thou art neither hot nor cold I will
spew thee out of my mouth,' he could scarcely head
a group. The word 'trimmer', cast at him as a re-
proach, he wore proudly as an emblem, and though
he understood his fellows, he would not be genial
with them, despising the promiscuity of the common
idol as much as the 'wet popularity' of the jovial
companion. Aristocratic and sceptical, with something of the weight of disillusion hanging about him,
hating to ally himself with a party lest it should injure
those precious things it declared itself created to
preserve, he stands a slightly lonely figure amid the
noisy, brutal, strife and bustle of his time. On the
other hand, he illuminates it with his sure wisdom,
couched in an epigrammatic prose which for balance
and modulation might, except for an occasional
metallic ring, have served as a model for Congreve.

It may not even be going too far to wonder
whether he would not have preferred only to illumi-
nate rather than take an active part in the decisive
events of the crucial period in which he lived. 'Not-
withstanding my passion for the town,' he wrote to
his brother Henry, himself a politician, and Roches-
ter's blithe correspondent, 'I dream of the country as
men do of small beer when they are in a fever.' But
more significant are some of his *Moral Thoughts and*

Reflections: 'The Government of the World is a great thing; but it is a very coarse one too, compared with the Fineness of Speculative Knowledge'; and 'Men make it such a Point of Honour to be fit for Business, that they forget to examine whether Business is fit for a Man of Sense'. But his scepticism is double-edged; here too, he trims, as it were, the boat of his own personality: 'A little Learning *misleadeth*, and a great deal often *stupifieth* the Understanding,' and then, immediately, 'Great Reading, without applying it, is like Corn *heaped* that is not *stirred*, it groweth musty'. All the while, in his inner life as well as in his political career, we feel him poised between two extremes, seeking the mean, not so much as an ideal in itself as being the only way to keep his independence. 'A man may dwell so long upon a Thought, that it may take him prisoner'; he may become a slave as much to an idea as to a party. Yet here again we meet complexity within complexity, proviso set against proviso; independence may not be the best way to serenity, since 'Happy those who are convinced so as to be of the general Opinions'. He was as far as can be from his own incisive definition of a fool as one who hath no dialogue within himself.

It is not surprising that to plain men like Clarendon, or to Bishop Burnet, who in his busy certitude can have had very little time for dialogue within himself, Savile seemed a puzzle and a paradox. Men are always inclined to condemn those who do not fit conveniently into a category: they are continually suspicious of those who appear at one moment honestly to agree with them and the next as honestly to differ. Nothing is harder for a man than to see his own inconsistency; his conviction of the oneness of his being seems in itself enough to unify his opinions. But we who are free of the tempers of the Rebellion and the Revolution can judge that Halifax never varied from himself. 'With relation to the public,' Burnet justly remarked, 'he went backwards and forwards, and changed sides so often, that in conclusion no side trusted him.' But of course, it was the public which oscillated from boundary to boundary, and Macaulay finally answered Burnet:

He was called inconstant, because the relative position in which he stood to the contending factions was perpetually varying. As well might the pole-star be called inconstant because it is sometimes to the east and sometimes to the west of the pointers.

The truth is, he was staunch to principles Burnet could not possibly appreciate, the principles of political growth and adaptability, which again confirmed his toleration. It is easy enough to be a last dyker; 'constancy will be thought a virtue even when it is a mistake; and the ill-Judging World will be apt to think that Opinion most right, which produceth the greatest number of those who are willing to suffer for it.' It is far harder so to discipline and refine thought that it can be applied afresh, like a new yet tried instrument, to every new-born problem that emerges. Thus, to the vulgar view, to have been the cause of defeating the Exclusion Bill must have committed Savile to opposing William's sovereignty; yet it is admitted that, if the measures passed at the Revolution bear the stamp of any one mind, it is the Trimmer's. To counsel tolerance yet to warn dissenters against the Indulgence once more looks contradictory; to 'seem full of commonwealth notions' yet to go into 'the worst part of King Charles's reign', mere levity. Yet Savile was acting only at the dictates of a superior discernment, testing everything by his own rigorous thought, his own sifted experience; and posterity has judged him in the main right. If he did go into the worst part of King Charles's reign, by which, presumably, Burnet meant the issue of the *Quo warranto* writs during the Tory reaction after the Popish Plot, which deprived many corporations of their charters, he may have done so lest worse should befall. Even a Whig may allow that there may be much truth in Dryden's partisan praise in the dedication of *King Arthur* to Halifax:

So many Wives, who have yet their Husbands in their Arms: so many Parents, who have not the number of their Children lessen'd: so many Villages, Towns and Cities, whose Inhabitants are not decreased, their Property violated, or their Wealth diminished, are yet owing to the sober Conduct, and happy results of your Advice.

To us the real puzzle is why Halifax, with a nature largely contemplative, owning Montaigne to be his favourite author, should have gone into politics at all: why, like Sir William Temple, he did not cultivate his garden, or, like Evelyn, busy himself with the higher frivolities of the mind. And here we too may fail to understand unless we take account of his extraordinary complexity, extraordinary, not because he was diverse—nearly all lesser men are diverse, are lesser perhaps because of their diversity—but that being so divided he was yet so powerful in politics, so chastened, so castigated in prose.

That with his rank and high connexions, his wealth and his wit, he should in youth have wanted to engage in the traffic of the world is natural enough; perhaps, even, he found it the best field for his wit, which he brought unchained to the council table. It cost him his place there once, when he described Danby's manner in refusing a bribe as 'strangely like that of a man who, being asked to give another the use of his wife, declined in terms of great civility'. His wisdom was not for the study alone: he carried it with him, as all true wisdom should be carried, in his pocket. 'One great argument', a contemporary said of him, 'of the prodigious depth and quickness of his sense is that many of his observations and wise sayings were on the sudden, when talking to a friend, or going from him.' If, as Evelyn remarked, he was 'in his younger days somewhat positive', that is only evidence that he had already acquired his talent for pithy statement, which must always seem a little one-sided. All goes to show that with his great charm, which at once seduced Charles, who had been hostile to him on his reputation, he was fitted for the commerce of the world.

Nevertheless, it is equally clear that he soon came to despise it. 'It is the Fools and Knaves that make the Wheels of the World turn. *They* are the *World*; those few who have Sense or Honesty sneak up and down single, but never go in Herds.' Again, 'To understand the World, and to like it, are two things not easy to be reconciled.' Worse than contempt, disillusion overtook him: 'It is a Misfortune for a Man not to have a Friend in the World, but for that reason he shall have no Enemy.' Thus we are led to the conclusion that it was patriotism pure and simple which kept him in the service of the State. 'There is a Smell in our Native Earth better than all the Perfumes in the East'; the Trimmer 'would rather die, than see a spire of *English* Grass trampled down by a Foreign Trespasser'. Yet patriotism alone will not account for his choice: Temple, too, was a patriot, but retired to Moor Park. Therefore we are made to think that it was a real intellectual distaste for extremes which kept him in the dusty market-place, that passion for liberty which he ascribes to the Trimmer. Wealth he did not need, power he did not want—not, at least, enough to sacrifice his integrity for its sake; but he could not bear to see the Government in the hands of 'small dabblers in Conjuring, that raise up angry Apparitions to keep Men from being reconcil'd, like Wasps that fly up and down, buz and sting to keep Men unquiet'. There was need for Trimmers; it was necessary to step into the breach if the laws were to be preserved and fulfil their proper function.

In *The Observator* of 3 December 1684, where Roger l'Estrange attacked the policy of moderation, a Trimmer is declared to be

a man of latitude, as well in politics as in divinity; a kind of comprehensive Christian that makes more a conscience of indulging a division from the Church than of preserving unity in it. He has more charity for the transgressors of a law, than for the observers of it, more for the offence than for the constitution. . . . He takes away the rule that the people may not break it.

It was just on this point that Savile could take him up. After the preface, in which he defines the Trimmer's balancing position, he opens by saying, 'Our Trimmer, as he hath a great Veneration for Laws in general, so he hath more particularly for our own'; and the first section, which is the longest of all, is devoted to the exposition of this attitude. Like Coke, he saw in the laws the surest safeguards of liberty, and later suffered his name to be struck off the list of Councillors by James II rather than tolerate the repeal of the Habeas Corpus and Test Acts. Our Trimmer, 'as he thinketh the Laws are Jewels, so he believeth that they are nowhere better set than in the constitution of our *English* Government, if rightfully understood, and carefully preserved'. But he was no rigid doctrinaire, and he followed this remark at once with: 'It would be too great Partiality to say they are perfect or liable to no Objection; such things are not of this world; but if they have more Excellencies and fewer Faults than any other we know, it is enough to recommend them to our esteem.' What disgusted him was to see them 'Mangled, Disguised, Speak quite another language than their own, to see them thrown from the Dignity of protecting Mankind to the disgraceful Office of destroying them'. Developing this thought further in answering l'Estrange, he blamed the Church, not for its principles, but for a too busy diligence, for excessive zeal which did it no service, and was 'troubled to see Men of all sides sick of a Calenture of a mistaken Devotion'.

The Character of a Trimmer, written largely for the Royal eye, is the best known of Savile's writings; but that which had the greatest effect in his day, being distributed in thousands, was *A Letter to a Dissenter*. It is a brilliant piece of writing, pondered and decisive, profound yet never dull, drawing its images in the happiest way from everyday things in workaday expressions. 'You are therefore to be hugged now, only that you may be the better squeezed at another time.' He never indulges in polemics, he never raises his voice; his argument proceeds calmly, inexorably, yet almost with an air of affability in its sweet reasonableness. If ever prose had the quality of persuasiveness it is Savile's. Nevertheless, in its perfect yet deadly temper we are reminded of *A Modest Proposal*. *The Anatomy of an Equivalent*, with which he followed it up, is as good; and he points out in a phrase what others would have taken pages to explain, that 'There is no bartering with *Infallibility*.' His *Cautions for Choice of Members of Parliament* is as fresh to-day as at the elections for which it was written. He is against carpet-baggers; popularity-mongers; the poor and ambitious; he deplores the choice of 'slight Airy Men', but the dislike of them 'must not go so far, as to recommend heaviness in opposition to it'. He would have few lawyers, for 'they are Men used to argue on both sides of a question'—a view which reminds us of a not far distant controversy. He would have members neither too young nor too old: 'It would be well for the Business of the World, if young Men would stay longer before they went into it, and old men not so long before they went out of it.' His shafts against party are as keen as any of Swift's, and are as true to-day as when he wrote them; but we may be sure that, had he lived when the system was in operation, he would have accepted it as a natural growth and made all possible use of it. Sturdy as he was against party, there is one maxim of his, usually overlooked, where he says as much. 'If there are two parties,' he wrote in *Political Thoughts and Reflections*, 'a Man ought to adhere to that which he disliketh least, though on the whole he doth not approve of it: For whilst he doth not list himself in one or the other Party, he is looked upon as such a Straggler, that he is fallen upon by both.' His conclusion is tinged with that melancholy, never soft, but hardened by judgement, which runs through so much of his writing. Having given his opinions who ought not to be chosen, he closes: 'If I should be ask'd, who ought to be, my Answer must be, Chuse *Englishmen*; and when I have said that, to deal honestly, I will not undertake that they are easy to be found.' His last political tract, *A Rough Draught of a New Model at Sea*, written in 1694, has lost its interest because all that he proposed has long since been accepted, namely that gentlemen who hold commissions at sea must be 'tarpaulins' too, trained in their craft, so that 'they may have a Right to be admitted free *Denizens* of *Wapping*'. Yet there is one famous phrase, which may sound in the ears of those entrusted with our hopes at Disarmament Conferences:

It may be said now to *England, Martha, Martha,* thou

art busy about many things, but one thing is necessary. To the Question, What shall we do to be saved in this World? there is no other Answer than this, Looke to your Moate.

Halifax has been described as 'the most subtle and original thinker of the Restoration era', and this claim rests on the fact that he regarded the State, not as an artificial thing, but as a growing organism; its rule not as an exercise for theoreticians, but as a problem for the experience of men to solve. If he harks back to Coke in his love of law, he casts forward to Burke, not only in details, as in the fit treatment of the American colonies, but in general conception, in his conviction that nothing would stand which did not stand upon its own merits. It was, for instance, no love of James which made him fight so dazzlingly against the Exclusion Bill, speaking some thirteen times in a debate which lasted more than six hours, answering clause by clause the brilliant thrusts of his uncle Shaftesbury, the cunning arguments of his brother-in-law Sunderland, while Charles stood languidly by the fireplace:

> *Jotham* of piercing Wit and pregnant Thought,
> Endew'd by nature and by learning taught
> To move assemblies, who but only tri'd
> The worse a while, then chose the better side;
> Nor chose alone, but turn'd the balance too;
> So much the weight of one brave man can do.

It was his fear of change, his dislike of introducing a new principle, which made him choose the 'better side'.

He was no believer in violent methods. 'A rooted Disease must be *stroaked away*, rather than *kicked away*,' he wrote in *Miscellaneous Thoughts and Reflections*. 'Desiring to have any thing mended, is venturing to have it spoiled. To know when to let Things alone is a high pitch of good Sense. But a Fool hath an Eagerness, like a Monkey in a Glass Shop, to break every thing in handling.' That is almost pure Burke. This view may excuse his inaction, for which he has been blamed, when events were moving to a crisis under James; for if he saw which way they were tending, it was no affair of law-keepers to hasten what must naturally arrive. But when William did come, and James fled, then he was nothing if not decisive. He 'had not been privy to the prince's coming', he told Reresby, 'but now he was here, and on so good an occasion,' it was plain that he must be supported. For, to go back to his *Political Thoughts*,

A Constitution cannot make itself; some body made it, not at once, but at several times. It is alterable; and by that draweth nearer Perfection; and without suiting itself to differing Time and Circumstances, it could not live. Its Life is prolonged by changing seasonably the several Parts of it at several times.

Again that is Burke; both men would lead reform, but both would all the while protest against innovation.

If we turn to those of Savile's works which may come more properly under the heading of literature than of politics, namely, some of the 'Maxims', *Advice to a Daughter*, and *The Character of Charles II*, we find the same qualities at once of moderation and of epigram. The moderation is all the more surprising in the maxims—on the whole a tedious form of literature for the very reason that it makes for one-sidedness and over-statement, and in which a very small modicum of truth may froth into a monstrous deal of saucy wit. There, more than in any other mode of writing, it is not the fact, but the point of view, which tells; but with Savile we never lose sight of the former. He has been compared with La Rochefoucauld (Vauvenargues might have been a nearer parallel), but he is better than La Roche-foucauld. Turn to one of the latter's most famous pronouncements, 'La gravité est un mystère du corps, inventé pour cacher les défauts de l'esprit.' That is only half true, but the following is wholly so: 'A little Vanity may be allowed in a Man's Train, but it must not sit down at Table with him.' Or take the intolerable cynicism, the palpable falsehood, of 'Ce que les hommes ont nommé amitié n'est qu'une société, un ménagement réciproque d'interêt, un échange de bons offices; ce n'est enfin qu'un com-merce où l'amour propre se propose toujours quelque chose à gagner,' and compare it with the humanity, the generosity, the wisdom of 'Friendship cannot live with Ceremony, nor without Civility'. There is hardly one of his sayings that is cheap, though some are not encouraging: 'It is a dangerous thing to guess partially, and a melancholy thing to guess right'; but it would be false to say they do not make for courage. 'A Difficulty raiseth the Spirits of a Great Man, he hath a mind to wrestle with it, and give it a Fall. A Man's mind must be very low, if the Difficulty doth not make a part of his Pleasure.' Nor, cautious as Halifax was, is he always for caution.

'A Man hath too little Heart, or Wit, or Courage, if
he hath not sometimes more than he should'; and
then he allows himself a touch of dinner-table smart-
ness: 'Just enough of a good thing is always too
little.' Again, there is the often quoted 'A Man
throweth himself down whilst he complaineth; and
when a Man throweth himself down, nobody goeth
to take him up again.' His maxims are the reflections,
not of a recluse, nor of a disappointed and embittered
man, but of one nourished by experience, who had
been powerful in the affairs of the world and accorded
the highest of its honours.

The Character of Charles II is admittedly a master-
piece. He views his late sovereign with detachment
but affection, always tracing the reason for his faults
but, though understanding them, not excusing them.
It is a statement written by an intimate whose business it was to protect and guide as much as to watch
and sum up. The latter, however, he did, and is
amazingly skilful in analysing what are apparently
the most insignificant actions:

The thing called *Sauntering* is a stronger Temptation to
Princes than it is to others. The being galled with Importu-
nities, pursued from one Room to another with asking Faces;
the dismal Sound of unreasonable Complaints, and ill-grounded
Pretences; the Deformity of Fraud ill-disguised; all these
would make any Man run away from them; and I used to
think it was the Motive for making him walk so fast. So it
was more properly taking Sanctuary.

On the King's mistresses Savile is most entertaining,
not blaming Charles overmuch, once admitted that
in his make-up he had 'as little of the *Seraphick* part

as ever Man had'. 'Of a Man who was capable of choosing, he chose as seldom as any Man that ever lived.' Indeed, his lack of selection is the main charge against him, and once, perhaps, we hear a personal note: 'But of all Men that ever *liked* those who *had Wit*, he could best *endure* those who had *none*.' But always, when he can, Savile brings his observation of the particular fact into the realm of generalization:

He was so good at finding out other Men's weak Sides, that it made him less intent to cure his own: That generally happeneth. It may be called a treacherous Talent, for it betrayeth a Man to forget to judge himself, by being so eager to censure others: This doth so misguide Men the first Part of their Lives, that the Habit of it is not easily recovered, when the greater Ripeness of their Judgement inclineth them to look more into themselves than into other Men.

Men love to see themselves in the false Looking-glass of other Men's Failings. It maketh a Man think well of himself at the time, and by sending his Thoughts abroad to get Food for Laughing, they are less at leisure to see Faults at home. Men choose rather to make War in another Country, than to keep all well at home.

He was not, however, concerned to blame, and his last paragraph may resume his whole intention. 'Let his Royal Ashes then lie soft upon him, and cover him from harsh and unkind Censures; which, though they should not be unjust, can never clear themselves from being indecent.'

The work, perhaps, which most endears him to us is the delicious *Advice to a Daughter*. It is a gay document, bubbling with laughter, but imbued with all the seriousness of a real paternal love. It is shot with sadness, and all the while seems to indicate, rather than the delights of life, the way of making the best of a bad job. It would not have surprised him, but it would have hurt him, to read the 'Labour wasted' somebody wrote on the flyleaf of his daughter's copy—the daughter whose son was the famous Lord Chesterfield. It has all the wit and balance of the best of his writings; and if the wisdom is worldly, it is as if he knew that that is the only wisdom which can be imparted. Saints are not made by precept; shining examples are born, not constructed out of advice, or manufactured out of books. Nevertheless, his teaching throughout is of the most palatable sort of worldliness; he is far from preaching success or flashiness or gain. Here, as everywhere, he is moderate and tolerant, and all the while we feel his solicitude for the happiness of his daughter, his wistfulness that she should be everything that is best in the fine tradition of the English gentlewoman. He might well say: 'Whether my skill can draw the Picture of a fine Woman, may be a question; but it can be none, That I have drawn that of a kind Father.'

In everything he warns her against excess:

The next thing to be observ'd to you is, That *Religion* doth as little consist in loud Answers and devout Convulsions at Church, or Praying in an extraordinary manner. Some ladies are so extream stirring at *Church*, that one would swear the *Worm* in their *Conscience* made them so unquiet. Others will have such a Divided Face between a *Devout Goggle* and an *Inviting Glance*, that the unnatural Mixture maketh even the *best Looks* to be at that time *ridiculous*.

He is admirable in his advice lest she should happen upon an unworthy husband, in his remarks upon the treatment of servants, who are to be looked upon as humble friends, in her manner of speech, of dress, of diversions. There is nothing in it that is out of date, excepting in external details. And his method is always to turn the gentle beam of laughter, not the fierce ray of satire, upon the things he wishes to warn his daughter against, feeling that here more than anywhere it is necessary to amuse if wisdom is to follow upon his admonishment.

And if in his works our minds are kept refreshed and alert by the vivacity of his descriptions, the justice of his wit, the homeliness of his allusions, so again and again the ear is delighted with the exactness, the liveliness, the colour of his phrasing. Indeed, he is often too balanced and antithetical. Continuous epigram is apt to become staccato and destroy the wholeness of the paragraph: over-polish seems sometimes to detract from the naturalness of utterance, even where polish itself is natural. But when Halifax is moved he flows out into something more stately, more warm; his emotion informs the paragraph and gives it a more arterial structure. One notable instance, where the emotion is tenderness, may be found in the penultimate paragraph of *Advice to a Daughter*; but a less personal spirit, a spirit which seems to speak with the tongue of a nation rousing itself from sleep, is the life-blood of the one from *The Character of a Trimmer*, which begins:

I say when our *Trimmer* representeth to his Mind, our Roses blasted and discolour'd, whilst the Lilies Triumph and grow insolent upon the Comparison; when he considereth our own once flourishing Lawrel, now withered and dying, and nothing left us but a remembrance of a better part in History than we shall make in the next Age, which will be no more to us than an Escutcheon hung upon our Door when we are dead; when he foreseeth from hence growing Infamy from abroad, confusion at home, and all this without the possibility of a Cure, in respect of the voluntary fetters good Men put upon themselves by their Allegiance; without a good measure of preventing Grace, he would be tempted to go out of the world like a *Roman* philosopher, rather than endure the burthen of Life under such a discouraging Prospect.

If only for his firm and independent conscience, apart from his clearness of thought and his high courage, Halifax deserves to be remembered with respect and admiration. He might have been a Restoration wit, he chose to be a counsellor of kings: he might have led a party, he elected to be trusted by none. If he loved the pomp and tinsel of position well enough, he was never self-seeking, and dared to disagree with his masters as well as to flout the mob. If, on the one hand, he went into the worst part of King Charles's reign, on the other he tried to save Stafford and Russell; he went bail for Marlborough when he was in disgrace. But he is above all a winning figure, a full man, free and self-contained, virile and sagacious, never condescending yet always friendly, holding ever a little apart as though aware that, however active one may be in the world, to keep within oneself those things of the spirit best worth the holding exacts the heavy but not intolerable price of loneliness and misprision.

III

BUNYAN'S MR. BADMAN

JOHN BUNYAN, who was born in 1628 and lived until 1688, just missing the Revolution, was a more prolific writer than most of us suppose. Pamphlet after pamphlet poured out from the abundant pen of the tinker, who aroused a certain degree of ire because he 'mended souls as well as pots and pans'. Employed enough in his early years, partly in being a bold dog (though this does not seem to have amounted to much, blasphemy apart; he cannot hold a candle to St. Augustine for meritorious profligacy), and partly with fighting in the Great Rebellion, almost certainly on the Cromwellian side, he turned seriously to writing only when years of prison for illicit preaching brought him leisure. He is known chiefly by his three great works, *Grace Abounding*, *The Pilgrim's Progress*, and *The Holy War*. Yet *Mr. Badman*, written in 1680, two years after *The Pilgrim's Progress*, *Part I*, and two before *The Holy War*, deserves to live, even though the picture 'of a vulgar, middle-class, unprincipled scoundrel', 'travelling along the primrose path to the everlasting bonfire', as Froude put it, is not in itself a very attractive subject. But 'Bishop Bunyan' understood what he was about. He knew not only how to wield a pen, but also when to unsheathe it: and if his admonitions do not now strike home as once they did, there is enough of the universal in them to give point to his incisive and well-balanced prose.

It would be doing Bunyan a grave disservice to attempt to argue that *The Life and Death of Mr. Badman* is a book at all on the same level as *The Pilgrim's Progress* or *Grace Abounding*, both of them works of very profound scope, portentous works, declaring, as Mr. Chesterton has claimed, that religion is 'a terror, a splendour, a necessity, and a nuisance'. It has not the fiery prophetic quality of those early works, which makes them stand out so amazingly from the pious literature of the period. It is true that here Bunyan is a prophet so far as to cry 'Ichabod' in his preface, but there are people in every age who utter aloud: 'Yea, our earth reels and staggereth to and fro like a Drunkard, the transgression thereof is heavy upon it.' There seems, however, a great deal of ruin left in the earth, and it is not that familiar sound which makes us lend an attentive ear to what Bunyan has to say in *Mr. Badman*. What attracts us is the human element, rather than the divine, the knowledge of life, and the bracing virility, both in the matter of the tale and in the telling of it.

Almost without being aware, we are led into the human world which Bunyan knew, in which he had been brought up, and from which he most readily drew his moral illustrations. We are plunged into the life of non-conformity, and unwittingly accept its judgements and values. We come to share its view of informers against meetings, of hypocritical 'professors', and, let us say it straightway, of dishonest tradesmen. If the greater works are too deep-rooted in prehistoric impulse, in primitive reactions, in, if you like to go with Mr. Chesterton, too 'barbaric' conceptions to maintain religion as a cog in civilization, this is not true of *Mr. Badman*. It does not, certainly, appeal to a high and complex order of society, like the writings of Jeremy Taylor; it does not declare itself written for a sect, like the *No Cross, No Crown* of William Penn; but it is definitely written for and about a class, the trading class, the class of 'chapmen', to which Bunyan's father belonged. His more famous earlier book was 'written concerning the Progress of the Pilgrim from this World to Glory'; but though Bunyan declared at the beginning of his preface that Mr. Badman's career would illustrate the 'Life and Death of the Ungodly, and of their travel from this world to Hell', in truth, it is much more a guide how to live decently and respectably in this world. The later book is not a pendant to or completion of the first, as Dante's *Paradiso* is to his *Purgatorio*; as *Paradise Regained* is to *Paradise Lost*. The books are as different from one another as the retailing of a dream should be from the recounting of facts. Thus, if we are made to feel that false weights and measures are abhorrent to God, a thesis sustained with much scriptural quotation, we are also made to realize quite clearly that such behaviour is very bad for trade. It is driven well home to us that one of Mr. Badman's worst offences was sham bankruptcy. In the same way, though uncleanness is inveighed against with much weighty textual authority, we are more impressed by the fact that it ruins the body than by the other truth that it corrodes the spirit. A whore is a deep pit; but the dread result of Mr. Badman's taking one for his second wife was not so much that it weakened his soul as that it wasted his substance. The whole book, in short, is much more a worldly warning than a spiritual exhortation.

The Pilgrim's Progress we all apply to ourselves, whatever our creed, if we try to walk in any sort of spiritual road, be it never so humble and unassuming; the allegory works into us whatever mode of life we pursue. The fears of Christian are our fears, his hopes and despairs ours also; we meet the same obstacles, human or inanimate: but unless we actually use false measures, or are markedly incontinent, or scurrilously blasphemous, we do not think of applying the lessons of Mr. Badman to ourselves. If we transgress in any of these ways the story is certainly a sad warning; we will do well to pay heed—and at any rate the attention of our neighbour and his sons ought to be drawn to it. The point, not to labour it, is that *The Pilgrim's Progress* is universal, and *Mr. Badman* is not.

The little treatise is put in the form of a dialogue, he tells us, 'that I might with more ease to myself, and pleasure to the Reader, perform the work'. He was not the first to use this form for pietistic purposes, and it was not even his own first attempt at it, since among his earlier works is to be found the dialogue called *Profitable Meditations*, while *The Pilgrim's Progress* is partly in that form. Nevertheless, it was an ingenious idea to cast this work so. As a plain narrative it would not have admitted of either the pious digressions or the picturesque illustration; as a sermon it could not fail to be tedious. And not only do we stand the sermonizing for the sake of the inset pictures, but also for the sake of the company we find ourselves in. Two rather pompous, and, one may as well confess it, rather prosy old worthies, sit under a tree, armed with righteousness and a good store of texts, to tell each other what we all of us already know. Mr. Wiseman (the name is not this time attached to Worldly, but we suspect the namesakes to be cousins) proceeds to tell Mr. Attentive all about Mr. Badman, from which there flows a generous stream of comment, aided by question and answer, and anecdotes illustrative of sudden judgement. But for us, who are not Calvinists in reason, even if some of us may be so in temper, much of the force is robbed from the example when we learn that the unlucky man was 'infected with Original corruption' and 'came polluted into the world'. He was certainly a horrid little boy, but we can understand his desire to escape what were obviously the terribly dreary Sundays he was expected to live through. Yet, all the same, there is something rather lovable about these two old gossips, and they are not drawn without a certain humour, though whether Bunyan was aware of this is perhaps doubtful. When Wiseman tells Attentive that Badman has suffered a fearful death, the latter is all agog to hear about it. Wiseman insists on first telling him the story of the wretched man's life, and Attentive has to agree to listen; 'but', he adds, 'be as brief as you can, for I long to hear the manner of his death'.

Thus, even if Bunyan was not altogether aware of the humour he was infusing into his moral tale, he evidently took into account the frailty of the average reader, who then, as now, liked to feel his flesh creep. The love of horror is never absent from man's make-up, and he is ready to indulge it anywhere, in a sermon of Donne's as much as in a play of Webster's: and if Dean Inge to-day does not attempt to vie with the Grand Guignol, it is by no means certain that he would not be well advised to do so. Bunyan, at any rate, persuades his reader to follow the tale by promising him a sugar-plum at the end—and then disappoints him. Instead of a Faustus-like death, instead of terrors and shrieks, of devils with red-hot pincers, and all the paraphernalia of seventeenth-century satanic imagery, we learn that Mr. Badman 'died like a Lamb', 'like a Chrisom Child'. We fail to be impressed by the fact that this makes his end all the more dreadful, since this calmness precluded the possibility of a death-bed repentance. Indeed, Bunyan appears to have been afraid that this might be so, thus we hear by the way of people being ravished from the earth by devils, of being swallowed up in the ground, and of being cut off suddenly in sinful pride; and he precedes the end of Mr. Badman by the account of the death of one John Cox, in which he describes, with curiously revolting realism, one of the most horrible suicides that can be imagined. The dramatic effect of the serene death after the gruesome one is strong enough; Bunyan seems to say, 'Well, if you wanted physical horrors, here you are, and I hope you like them; but I can show you something far worse by way of spiritual horror in this ox-like death'. Yet the suspicion lurks that he felt the need of something sensational, if not for himself, at least to impress his reader.

The style of this book is recognizably Bunyan's, if it has not quite the perfect simplicity of *The Pilgrim's Progress*. It is the same voice, with its Biblical intonation, its love of the plain phrase, its sparing use of the long word. But being more polemical, the long words creep in more often. Take this from *Mr. Badman*:

> Here now is a prohibition, plainly forbidding the Believer to marry with the Unbeliever, therefore they should not do it. Again, these unwarrantable Marriages, are, I may so say, condemned by *irrational* creatures, who will not couple but with their own sort. Will the *Sheep* couple with the *Dog* . . .? &c.

The argument is weak, it will not hold water physiologically; but the point is, the style is weaker than, say, this from *The Pilgrim's Progress*:

> To talk of things that are good, to me is very acceptable, with you or with any other; and I am glad that I have met with those that incline to so good a work.

Both passages are hit upon much at random, but the comparison will hold good throughout; the later tale is not quite so sure as the earlier one. We are down to the earth, which is not so solid as the imagination. It is still a good style, but it is no longer the impeccable homespun. Yet, to note the differences between Bunyan and others writing in much the same vein, let us look for a moment at two other excellent styles; first Penn's, which would not have suited Bunyan, who disapproved of the mystic element in Quakerism that afterwards made so dangerous an appeal to William Law:

So I say to thee, unless thou believest, that he that stands at the door of thy heart and knocks, and sets thy sins in order before thee, and calls thee to acceptance, be the Saviour of the world, thou wilt die in thy sins, and where he is gone, thou wilt never come. If thou believest not in him, it is impossible that he should do thee any good, or effect thy salvation: Christ works not against faith, but by it. It is said of old, 'he did not many mighty works in some places, because the people believed not in him'. So that if thou truly believest in him, thine ear will be attentive to his voice in thee, and the door of thine heart will open to his knocks. Thou wilt yield to the discoveries of his light, and the teaching of his grace will be very dear to thee.

(No Cross, No Crown.)

The words are simple enough; the difference lies in the complexity with which they are woven, in their rhythm, which argues a higher complexity of thought. A greater contrast still is Jeremy Taylor. Take this from *Holy Dying*:

Treat thy nurses and servants sweetly, and as it becomes an obliged and a necessitous person. Remember, that thou art very troublesome to them; that they trouble not thee willingly; that they strive to do thee ease and benefit, that they wish it, and sigh and pray for it, and are glad if thou likest their attendance: that whatsoever is amiss, is thy disease, and the uneasiness of thy head or thy side, thy distemper or thy disaffections; and it will be an unhandsome injustice to be troublesome to them, because thou art so to thyself; to make them feel a part of thy sorrows, that thou mayest not bear them alone; evilly to requite their care by thy too curious and impartial wrangling and fretful spirit.

It is beautiful stuff, but very complicated; the matter is simple enough, but how courteous, how scholarly, how wise! It could not be applied to what Bunyan was trying to say, for Bunyan, indeed, is too hard upon the tempted. Having triumphantly weathered the storm, he has not enough sympathy for those who drive upon the rocks. He has no need, therefore, for gracefulness, but he is never gaunt, being soundly nourished upon the Bible. The recondite, even so much as was handy for Foxe in *The Book of Martyrs*, is of no service to him. His prose, in short, is chapman's prose, which, at its best, is something to be very proud of indeed. It is well shaped and muscular; it can do with precision what it sets out to do. It disdains nothing, and is afraid of nothing; it speaks with the directness and candour of the cottage fireside.

Indeed, there is a danger that we, reading it to-day, may find the interest of the book to reside largely in its quaintness, in its superstitious credulity, in its engaging artlessness. But no one can read it without being struck by the absolute honesty of the man who wrote it. This is really the quality which makes it worth reading, now and always. However we may differ in opinion, however much we may be turned away by the narrowness of the outlook, we cannot help responding to the wholeheartedness of Bunyan's speech. If here he is no longer the enrapt man of religion, if here he is

rather the practical shepherd who would lead us
into the fold, we cannot doubt the eagerness of his
aim. He is in a world besotted with vice, but he
will do what he can. He does not rage, nor bluster;
he will not sweep us off our feet in a tempest of
revivalist enthusiasm; he is not out to gain glory
for himself by his prayers for us (as Mrs. Badman
rather unpleasantly was by her prayers for her
husband); but partly to help us, and partly to
testify soberly to the truth. We may take it or
leave it; he will not hector us into heaven, nor ask
God to blow us there by the wind of His wrath.
It is, really, love that he offers us; and something
of the sweetness of George Herbert seems to per-
vade the grim old puritan, in spite of disappoint-
ment in life, and the apparent defeat of his cause.
He is not himself a bright and glorious saint; he
has not here the energy which gave swift wings to
the author of *The Pilgrim's Progress*; but he can
still persuade us, by his own virtue rather than by
his argument, that 'The Ornament and Beauty of
this lower World, next to God and his Wonders,
are the men that spangle and shine in godliness'.

IV

WILLIAM CONGREVE

I. *HIS LIFE*

THE biographer of Congreve has to deal with a skeleton of fact singularly bare of fleshly clothing. The main events of his life are known, the dates of his birth, his works, his employments, and his end; but around him has grown up a lamentably poor crop of such anecdote or tradition as makes it easy to fill out the limbs of his contemporaries. Literally all we know of Congreve is that he had a *tendre* for Mrs. Bracegirdle, that his wine was not always good, that he once had a mild temporary quarrel with Jacob Tonson; that he was a Whig and a Kit-cat with whom no Tory could disagree, and that towards the end of his life he was cared for by the second Duchess of Marlborough. Even malice, that invaluable sleuth-hound for the biographer, has had to content itself with distorting a silly tale of a meeting with Voltaire, and prying into the taciturn privacies of a will. Thus, in spite of a too portly person severely punished by gout, Congreve walks almost ghost-like through the vociferous times of King William and Queen Anne; and one can be tolerably certain that if little is known of his life it is because there is not much to know. Yet, not on account of the paucity of the material, but by reason of its quality, his character is clear as noonday. Where with Swift we have to probe a darkly complex being, with Pope a mind as deformed as his body, and with Addison to peer between the folds of a curtain he was studious to keep drawn, Congreve offers himself as a personality of rare gentleness and simplicity, wistfully desirous of pleasing and of ensuing peace.

He was born at Bardsley, near Leeds, in 1670, in the house of his great-uncle, Sir John Lewis. Though the Congreves were a family of considerable property, William's father, as a younger son, was an averagely poor army officer, who soon after his son's birth was appointed to command the garrison of Youghal, Co. Cork. Shortly afterwards he resigned, to become. the agent of the Earl of Cork, and lived at Lismore, whence he managed the Burlington properties. William's childhood was therefore passed in Ireland. He went to school at Kilkenny, where he may just have met Swift, and proceeded to Trinity College, Dublin, where he certainly knew the future Dean of St. Patrick's. At the end of 1688, Dublin being no place either for learning or for Protestants, both young men crossed to England, where Swift soon found a refuge with Sir William Temple. Congreve's father also left Ireland, since it was obviously useless to be agent in a land made desert by the Rapparees, and appears to have come into the family estates. Until 1691, when he became a law student, we know nothing more of Congreve, except that he was ill, and that he wrote his first play during convalescence in the country, also finding time to complete a novel which he brought up to town in his pocket.

He did not, apparently, much waste his energies

in studying at the Middle Temple: a young man with a stock of classical knowledge in his head and two manuscripts in his closet does not delight excessively in the diligent study of equity or torts, especially if he has an ample allowance. The coffee-house is his country, the publisher's room his goal. The latter was reached almost as easily as the former, for in 1691 *Incognita* was licensed, to be published early in 1692 under the pseudonym of *Cleophil*. It was a success, and was often reprinted. It certainly shows style and critical acumen; but its interest to us, apart from its undeniable charm, lies in the fact that in it Congreve reveals an important side of his nature, namely, the love of graceful living, a desire to poetize the rougher sides of life, or at least to withdraw himself from crudities, and dwell in a realm where politics and Pretenders did not exist, and nobody minded whether or no great captains pouched a few odd hundreds out of army contracts.

It was naturally upon the chocolate houses rather than upon Westminster Hall that Congreve made his attack, for in those informal clubs everybody met to discuss the news-sheet, the play, and his mistress, or to air his last cravat. There Whitehall met the city and Mirabell diced with Petulant: there non-juring parsons scanned with joy the latest news of English reverses on the continent, and Witwoud answered the call from a vizard in a chair. There Purcell might shock Dennis with a pun, and William Walsh 'drink' his tobacco while criticizing the verses read to him by Dr. Garth on the crying sins of apothecaries who would not give to the poor the nostrums in which he hardly believed. The final aim, of course, was to make one in the select circle at Will's, where Dryden ruled, and which was the haunt of such patrons as Lord Dorset and, indeed, of every one who was any one in the world of letters, provided he was not a personal enemy of the sometime laureate.

And soon, probably through his college friend Southerne, Congreve met Dryden, who was devoid of that jealousy old men sometimes feel towards their younger rivals, and liked to encourage any one who showed a budding talent. Congreve gave him his play to read, and Dryden was immensely struck: never, he declared, had he read such a brilliant first play. Bating a little alteration of certain points where Congreve erred owing to inexperience of the stage, it would do perfectly well. Accepted in 1692, and acted in 1693 by an all-star cast at Drury Lane, *The Old Bachelor* was a tremendous success, and ran for the unprecedented period of a fortnight. Congreve was at once hailed as a great genius; the legitimate successor of Dryden had at last appeared, as was attested by several laudatory poems. Now the world understood why Congreve had been chosen to write the complimentary verses prefatory to Dryden's *Persius*, a distinction his own translation of a Juvenal satire had not seemed to warrant. Never was a dawn more resplendent: and the sun which then rose never lost its brilliance in the eyes of the elect, in spite of certain dismaying moments caused by *The Tears of Amaryllis* or verses on the great Nassau. The latter, indeed, every aspirant to fame had to write as a sort of ticket of admission to the hall of letters: such things did not dim the brightness of the day.

The Double Dealer, acted in November 1693, was less successful. Sir Edmund Gosse suggested that the satire was too keen to be borne with equanimity by an audience of fops; but it is our acquaintance, not ourselves, we are apt to see on the stage, and we may guess that it was the introduction of a new, strangely melodramatic element in the work that caused its chilly reception, for the unfamiliar is never attractive to the pit. Congreve was innocent to be angry that a play so much better than his first should meet with so much less applause, but he was wise enough to cut out the most acid passages in his dedication to Montague. What is left is defiant enough, and his position was supported by Dryden's stout verses, in which Congreve is frankly, if foolishly, hoisted to the level of Shakespeare. The play was in the end successful, partly owing, perhaps, to Queen Mary's approval, and called forth the praises of Swift on 'his young Congreve'.

In 1694 Queen Mary died, and Congreve composed a poem on the event, *The Mourning Muse of Alexis*, in the smooth verses of which the poet a little overdid the artificiality Pope was to declare necessary to the pastoral form. Granting the validity of the kind of object Congreve tried to create, the poem is not badly done; but the form is barely tolerable to us now, and reflects only the last flicker of the flame that lighted Marvell and Cowley. And here we may take the opportunity to dispose of all Congreve's

occasional verse, which he continued to write until
about 1710. It is small beer, but it is as good as
anything printed between the death of Dryden in
1700 and the appearance of *The Rape of the Lock* in
1712, and it is often more scholarly. It certainly
has few competitors—the shocking ineptitudes
of Wycherley; Addison's tiresome *Campaign*; Tickell's redundant praises of 'the British Virgil', Addison to wit; the slender stock of Walsh; or the
pastimes, ponderous or slight, of the famous doctors,
and the nambypambyisms of 'pastoral Philips'. The
only verses which give much pleasure to-day are
those of Prior, who does not really better Congreve,
and the lighter sallies of Swift.

And since our present interest is Congreve's life
as a dramatist and a private person, we may here
summarily dispose also of his career as a civil servant,
which began at about this period. His posts, if not
quite sinecures, involved no arduous labours, and no
doubt he adequately discharged the duties of licenser
of hackney coaches, wine, and so forth, which in turn
fell to his lot. None of his posts was of great glory
or much emolument; and the only one which brought
at all a large income, or sounded tolerably well,
was that of Secretary to Jamaica, which was granted
him in 1715. Never indigent, his posts of £1,200
a year now made him passably rich, for he had some
private income, and the receipts of his plays and
poems.

The year 1694 was a stormy, quarrelsome one
for actors, and in 1695 some of the old Drury Lane
players, to whom Congreve allied himself, set up a

rival theatre in a converted tennis-court in Lincoln's
Inn Fields. It opened with *Love for Love*, his most
lively play, which, in spite of being a little too long,
was a triumphant success both in book form and on
the stage. The dramatist's reputation was thereby
enormously increased, and it was solidified in 1696
by the publication of Dennis's *Letters Upon Several
Occasions*, which contained the *Essay Upon Humour
in Comedy*. But, strange as it may seem to us, the
work that most swelled his fame with his contemporaries was his tragedy, *The Mourning Bride*,
produced early in 1697. It is a work that should
be approached by the modern reader with an open
mind, unprejudiced either by the contempt into
which it fell in the last century, or the unlucky
overpraise of Dr. Johnson. It repays reading at
least as much as the not unpleasing rants of Lee or
the insidious sighings of Rowe: it can hold its own
with *Oroonoko* and with some of Dryden. It has
about it a faint flavour of Racine, and is far above the
terrible fustian of such adaptations as *The Distrest
Mother*, as it is certainly more alive than *Cato*, which
displaced it in the public favour some seventeen
years later, for reasons not altogether aesthetic. At
any rate, as Sir Edmund Gosse pointed out, it has
great prosodic interest as a variation in the Miltonic
school. His contemporaries took it so much to
their bosoms that two passages at least are still
among our familiar quotations, even if the one about
a woman scorned really belongs to Brome, whose
work he must have studied carefully.

But Congreve's dramatic career was not to pass

untroubled, for in March 1698 a tornado which had been threatening for some two or three years burst upon play-going London in the form of Jeremy Collier and the famous *Short View of the Immorality and Profaneness of the English Stage.* That it should have caused so much perturbation seems to us comically exaggerated: to-day, theatrical London would regard such a work about as much as the Sunday dramatic societies are moved by the hortatory brayings of the Salvation Army band; but it fell like a thunderbolt in drawing-rooms, green-rooms, and chocolate-houses, while playmongers and morality-mongers wrestled noisily together in murky darkness. The reason, the reasonableness, and the result of the quarrel are too well known to need any discussion here. To-day, perhaps, one's sympathies are with both sides. We may, however, say something of Collier's attack and Congreve's reply.

The *Short View* was a muscular onslaught. It had not the polish of *The Character of a Trimmer*, nor the bare, if human, austerity of *Holy Dying*, but it had something of the qualities of both. To be less urbane, it was the queerest farrago of scholarship and clap-trap, now very much to the point, now leagues away from it. The playwrights, it said, showed vice in pleasing garb; their treatment of the clergy amounted to blasphemy; they were disrespectful of the peerage and of the *Poetics* of Aristotle. The book is violent, sharp, clever, stupid; it is written with panurgical exuberance and sleight of hand: it may be described as the Billingsgate of belles-lettres. It was almost as impossible for a man of letters to answer, as it was for Job to argue with the voice that spoke to him out of the whirlwind—if not for quite the same reason. Many tried to reply: Dennis in a book aimed far too high for the average reader; Vanbrugh with a deal of burly good sense and humour, but with too little shot; Wycherley (or Gildon) with an airy touch rendered harmless by anonymity; and, upon persuasion, by Congreve.

It was not the sort of thing he was fitted to do; but since Dryden refused to be bothered, he was the obvious man to captain the other side. He undertook the task reluctantly, but by no means so ineffectually as is usually stated, in *Amendments of Mr. Collier's False and Imperfect Citations*. Yet though he succeeded in making Collier look a fool to any one not in sympathy with the parson, he by no means rose to the height the occasion demanded, and, confining himself to his own case, sometimes sank below the level one expects from a man of taste and sensibility. The idle reader will certainly pass an amused hour over it, but as a general defence of comedy the retort is weak. It was easy enough to establish that raillery was a legitimate instrument of spiritual cleansing; Pascal had shown that even God did not disdain the means: but if it was the justification of comedy that it pointed the finger at wrongdoing, he did not prove that many writers of comedy had not used the finger to beckon too zestfully to audiences to come and see their characters doing wrong. Indeed, Congreve took his cue a little too much from Collier: he dissected him shrewdly, but his manner was too familiar, and even abusive. Perhaps for us one of the main interests of the pamphlet is in a completely side issue, namely, that it shows with what extreme care Congreve studied his astrological matter before writing *Love for Love*.

As a matter of historical fact the outburst of Collier and his friends had little effect upon the stage beyond causing a little discomfort: if Restoration comedy was replaced on the bookseller's shelves by a less outspoken kind, it continued to be the most popular in presentation. It was not Collier, but the growth of democracy and the rise of domestic drama that killed it, and it is almost certainly to these last that was due the chilly reception given *The Way of the World*, which Congreve produced in 1700. His preface explains the failure; the play was written for a circle of select spirits. There is a legend, perpetuated by Dr. Johnson and repeated by Mrs. Inchbald, that the author, roused to a towering rage, came before the curtain and upbraidingly told the audience that he would never write for them again. The story is possibly true, but it is unlikely, and in any case merely tells us that the failure of a play over which Congreve had expended so much 'care and pains' may have been one of the reasons for his virtual abandonment of the stage.

But the desertion was never formal—life is rarely so clear-cut as that—since his actors still expected work from him, and he certainly intended to write for the theatre Vanbrugh built in 1704, though he only contributed one act of *Squire Trelooby*. This was a version of *Monsieur de Pourceaugnac*, the other two acts being scribbled by Vanbrugh and Walsh,

of which he thought so little that he would not have
it printed. Apart from that he wrote a masque, *The
Judgement of Paris*. Prizes of £200 were offered for
the best musical settings, and various performances
were given in 1701.[1] It has been condemned as
poetry, but there is one observation to be made: that
is, that whenever Congreve wrote anything to be
set to music the words are particularly adaptable
to song: that he knew he was engaged in an especial
form which has its own requirements and laws is
clear from his preface to *Semele*: and no one who
has heard Arne's *Judgement of Paris* or Handel's
Semele will deny his success. The latter does not
appear to have been performed until 1744,[2] but it
was published in 1710 in the collected works, and
it is this last date rather than 1700 that should be
given for his final abandonment of literary work.

Nevertheless, the history of his life from the
beginning of the century to his death is not of what
he did so much as of what was given him. The
important dates (except for the valuable essay on the
Pindaric Ode) are the ones when he got a new and
more lucrative quasi-sinecure; when Swift spoke
to Harley on his behalf; when Pope dedicated his
Iliad to him, or Steele his edition of *The Drummer*;
when Gay took him down to Bath. His life seems
merely a tale of growing infirmities—premature
obesity and cataract—symptoms of a gout-ridden

[1] Prizewinners: Eccles, Daniel Purcell, Finger, and Weldon. It is
usually stated that Eccles was first, but a claimant for Weldon has arisen.
See *The Times Literary Supplement*, 26th March, 1925.

[2] In a slightly adapted version. The famous song, 'Where'er you walk',
is, of course, Handel's interpolation from Pope's second pastoral.

frame, so that his account of having jumped twenty-one feet at his country place of Northall seems almost mythical. After 1710, apart from his edition of Dryden's works with its preface, and the *Epistle to Lord Cobham* written shortly before his death, he contributed nothing to literature, though perhaps the influence of his conversation on Swift, Pope, and Gay should not be allowed to count for nothing.

Yet his reputation grew with his age and infirmities: he was the man men of letters most liked to honour, perhaps because he had ceased to compete with them, and even withdrew himself from their society. He seems, indeed, to have had a predilection for feminine company, living with the Duchess of Marlborough, and calling forth such items of news as the following from Lady Suffolk to Mrs. Bradshaw (Bath, 19 Sept. 1721); 'Mrs. Berenger passes most of her time with Mr. Congreve, who is in the house with her.' At all events honour accrued, and when in 1729 he died as the result of a carriage accident, his body lay in state at Westminster, and his pall was carried by four peers of the realm.

There are three points about Congreve's life upon which his detractors never fail to seize, and which require comment: indeed, since his life was so uneventful, or at least so undocumented, they form real events of which two, in any other life, would have gone unregarded. They do, however, throw some light upon his character, even if they provide little to enable us to understand his work;

for though there is of necessity a connexion between a man's personality and his writings, in the case of so severely 'classical' a writer as Congreve, the threads are extremely difficult to lay bare. The points are: first, his abandonment of the stage; second, his famous remark to Voltaire, with which the first is intimately connected; and third, his meagre legacy to Mrs. Bracegirdle.

Macaulay, with an impercipience only to be explained by his prejudice, stated that Congreve ceased to write because he thought it beneath the dignity of a gentleman, an explanation as silly as his notion that Racine had, 'in conformity with the prevailing fashion, become devout, and given up writing for the theatre'. Macaulay was convinced that snobbery was the key to Congreve's character, simply because he moved in the same circles as every other man of letters, and because he preferred society which appreciated him. But in those days snobbery hardly existed, merely because it could not, the line between 'the quality' and the rest being too clearly defined. Tonson was not regarded in the same light as Tickell, who had at least a coat of arms, and Pope for years felt insecure of his position. So little, indeed, did the aristocracy despise writing, that they nearly all dabbled in it, and those who attained to any merit, such as Dorset, Halifax, or Lansdowne, made it their chief claim to distinction: and so far from writing being injurious to a man's position in society, it was only by their pens that such men as Prior attained any position in it at all. England was not like France where aristocracy was already being

invaded by the *nouveaux riches*, and study the comedy
of the period as we will, there is no George Dandin,
no Monsieur Jourdain in it. In any case, the point
does not arise with Congreve. It may be important
for the son of apothecary Pendennis, or for the off-
shoots of the great Mel, to insist upon their gentility,
as it is natural for a Cicero to be squeamish of his
fame; but that Congreve thought none of these
things necessary is made clear from the perfect
freedom with which he mingled in green-room circles.
He merely gravitated naturally to those places where
good food, good conversation, and graceful habits
were to be found.

It is probable that he ceased to write for the stage
for the obvious reasons, namely, on the one hand
that the compelling vitality was lacking, and on the
other that he had no impulsion to disburden himself
of a point of view, or communicate with his fellows
in that way. The first he seems to have exhausted,
not only in hard living, but in hard work: for its
quality, his output for the last ten years had been
enormous. He was already, in 1700, very sick and
sorry. As to the second, he had said all he had to say,
and had said it brilliantly, finally. And as for com-
municating with his fellows, the last time he had
tried to do so, they had misunderstood him. His
intimate friends could be counted upon not to do
that. What he had to give was only too evidently
wasted on the mob. Had Dryden not died, had
Mrs. Bracegirdle remained on the stage, he might
have been spurred, perhaps, to another play. But as
things were, what was the good?

After all, he may have thought, is there nothing else to be done in the world but write? Would not life be as well spent in organizing concerts, in musing upon the form of the Pindaric ode, and, above all, in 'feeling very sensibly and silently for those he loved', and in delighting them with his wit?

> Que les vers ne soient pas votre éternel emploi,
> Cultivez vos amis, soyez homme de foi:
> C'est peu d'être agréable et charmant dans un livre,
> Il faut savoir encore et converser et vivre,

Boileau had said, a plea Pope was to echo in his *Prologue to the Satires*. Did people not understand the enormous, blood-draining effort required in writing a good play? Values are not so easy to determine; and the value of a man is certainly not to be measured by the amount of ink he spills. Congreve stands out as the gentlest man of his period, always kindly, always helpful, who amongst his whole acquaintance did not number a single enemy.

He withdrew, then, from the battle of life, and posterity has impertinently declared that he had no right to do so. Unusually loved by his contemporaries, time has taken a foolish revenge, and there is a sneer in the judgement of the aloof, the urbane, the unruffled Mr. Congreve. It is remarkable how this attitude of serenity calls forth the dislike of mankind—Horatian is an adjective of contempt—as though it were intolerable vanity to pretend to that ease of mind for which everybody strives, and that nobody has any business to be successful in the art of possessing his soul in peace. Can a man be complete, it is asked, can he be human, who does not exhibit at least the unamiable weakness of irritability, in default of the virtue of hating? The business of philosophy may be to teach us how to die, it has no business to instruct us how to live. It is thus one evades the great common issues: it is not fair to keep out of the struggle, and assume airs of 'careless superiority'. Is there not always mankind to be bettered?

But there was much of the pagan about Congreve; his belief in the redemption of man was not strengthened by his knowledge of pre-Christian times. His semi-retirement suited his low vitality. He was not, like Swift, ambitious to be a great political power; he had no desire, like Addison, to be the perfect Christian man of the world, and *censor morum* to young ladies: he was not itching, like Pope, to have his finger in every pie. On the contrary, he wanted to be left alone, and he respected people enough to suppose they would appreciate the same treatment. He did not make demands on others, why should they make demands on him? One had no right to call one's desires standards, and expect others to live up to them, a point of view charmingly expressed in one of his happiest lyrics, 'False though she be to me and Love'. And whatever he may have suffered after his death in the matter of criticism, he certainly never censured others: the enemy to detraction earned the title of 'unreproachful man', readily allowing each that freedom of conscience posterity has begrudged him. He had a horror of forcing people to pretend to feelings they did not own; and this sentiment again he phrased felicitously in 'Tell me no more

I am deceiv'd'. It is, perhaps, one of the most scathing comments on the indelicacy of the Victorians that they saw fit to gibe at so attractive a man.

Then, one day, when

> retired without regret,
> Forgetting care, or striving to forget,
> In easy contemplation soothing time,

it was suddenly announced to him that the latest young literary star from France wished to be introduced to him. He would all at once have to engage in conversation with a young man, no doubt full of distressing eagerness, with whom he had no friends in common, and what was worse, no associations. None of those light allusions, none of that taking of things for granted which makes the company of friends so refreshing, would be possible. It would be a terrible effort. Why could not M. de Voltaire confine his lion-hunting to younger men, or to those who liked that kind of thing? He did not want to be added to the list. He would have to talk literature. He would be expected to discuss Juvenal, perhaps, and would be asked whether he thought Rapin had been altogether right on some controversial point. He would be on show. One knows, when one is fifty, what the young are: their energy, their terrific eagerness, leave one completely exhausted. As the fame-avid little man approached, half impudent, half fawning, his eyes shining with intelligence and snobbish delight, Congreve gathered himself together to meet him with his usual charm and instinctive dislike of rudeness. Soon M. de Voltaire made a reference to *The Way of the World*. Heavens! he was going to be asked to discuss his own work—or else he was going to be hideously flattered. He might be expected to explain some point about Millamant, and he had hardly thought about Millamant for twenty years. This must be stopped. M. de Voltaire, he said, must not expect to find in him a literary man: even if his plays were such as to merit M. de Voltaire's notice, which he was modest enough to doubt, he was afraid he could no longer lay claim to such pretensions: he must be regarded merely as a gentleman who lived simply, away from the complicated world of intellectuals. If M. de Voltaire found pleasure in the company of an oldish man, who, perhaps, was not lacking in culture and mental discernment, why, he would be very pleased.

But this, M. de Voltaire could not understand: if one had written a good thing, one had a right to be proud of it for the rest of one's life. What, otherwise, was the use of *la gloire*? When he was Congreve's age he knew better, but at the moment the older man's attitude seemed in some way derogatory of the calling of letters: his self-esteem was slightly wounded, and he rudely answered that Mr. Congreve was nothing to him, but that he had come to see the author of *The Way of the World*. So began that legend of what Johnson, himself with no mean respect for rank, has described as 'despicable foppery', and the obviously absurd notion that Congreve despised literature. Who in that famous meeting was the snob may admit of controversy, and some will be ready to agree with Lamb that 'the impertinent Frenchman was properly answered'.

There remains the question of Congreve's will, in which he left £200 to Mrs. Bracegirdle, and £10,000 to the Duchess of Marlborough. It was nobody's business but Congreve's, and the point should never have been raised, because we can know nothing whatever about it. Dr. Johnson thought the money should have gone to his family; but the Reverend Dr. Young, of pious memory, thought it should have gone to Mrs. Bracegirdle. It is curious that it should never have occurred to Macaulay that he and Young were the scandal-mongers, for they thus insisted that Mrs. Bracegirdle was Congreve's mistress. Of this there is no proof whatever. Certainly he was very fond of her, but she was notoriously distant to admirers, and surely it is stretching circumstantial evidence too far to assume that because Congreve lived in the same street with her, he was therefore on a footing only a parson could sanctify. For all we know, and it appears quite likely, she was the very lady of the poem who could not make him a saint, and of whom he could not make a sinner. And in any case, supposing he had been *du dernier bien* with her, is that any reason why he should proclaim the fact in his will? Anne Bracegirdle was tender of her reputation, and would probably have been profoundly annoyed at such an advertisement of her intimate life. It is always possible that Congreve made some private arrangement for her.

With her larger legacy the Duchess of Marlborough bought a £7,000 necklace, and erected a tablet to the poet's memory in Westminster Abbey. She also had constructed, to keep her company in her solitude, a waxen image of her departed friend. It was life size: it had a place at table with her, its physician, and its gouty bandages; it even nodded when spoken to. What a waste! What would Congreve not have given to invent so sublime an extravagance for one of his comedies? But such things are not invented; they occur: and nature out-did in a 'humour' the creator even of Lady Wishfort, and of the stupendous deformities of Foresight.

WILLIAM CONGREVE

II. *HIS WORK*

SINCE the year 1698, when Jeremy Collier flung his fulminations into the strongholds of the English drama, it has been the habit to tag Restoration comedy with the epithet 'licentious'. Macaulay scrawled the word in flaming characters throughout a full-length essay; and Lamb, in elaborating his nimble excuse, admitted the black indictment. What has happened that to-day we can face without flinching the prospect of seeing a comedy by Wycherley, and that Congreve touches our emotions instead of seeming a monster of callousness?

The first thing to recognize is that Restoration comedy was not merely licentious, even if the adjective is useful in revealing that its chief subject is the intimate relations between men and women. It is a mistake to confuse subject with treatment; one might as well say that *Vanity Fair, Madame Bovary,* and *Crime and Punishment* are licentious, because the characters in those books do not behave with the perfect propriety of the ladies in *Cranford.* The truth is—perhaps it was this that really shocked the moralists—that the comedy written from 1660 to 1700 dealt somewhat coldly with human love and lust, something cavalierly with the marriage tie. For there are, in the main, two attitudes one can take up in face of man's inability to live up to his ideals: one that of amusement in the comic spirit, which implies that man's ideals need modification, or at least that his attitude towards them does; the other that of horror, which implies that man himself needs modification—a task in which the risks of failure are discouraging.

The comic writers of that time took for subject the relations between the sexes not only because it lends itself so easily to jest (the earliest recorded laughter is on this subject) but because at that time it was one of crying importance. This was due to the fact not so much that society was lax, as that it was experimental. And this is perhaps why so much of this work seems to speak very directly to us, for it is the expression of people endeavouring to readjust their values after a great upheaval, trying to see themselves clearly, not as they might wish to be, or as a previous generation had said they ought to be, but as they really were. There is an extraordinary ring of intellectual honesty about the comedy of this period, an attempt to get down to bed-rock in these matters, which we find in the previous age only, perhaps, in Chapman fully, though we see it partially in Marston. It is the prominence of this subject, and the manner in which it is treated, that makes Restoration comedy different from any other.

But if the social assumptions of the previous age were broken down, Charles II's courtiers made others of their own, because without assumptions of some kind on every point society cannot exist at all. Being leisured, they were much preoccupied with love: being sceptical, their emotions were of the first importance to them, for when man's communings with God cease to matter intensely to him, his personal relations are bound to gain significance. They took as established that passion and affection were separate things, and that it was foolish to confuse them; they looked upon love as a purely personal reaction, marriage as a social performance—and the writers of comedy dissected the resulting complications. Under the surface, of course, the normal life of social acceptance went on; but what flared before the public eye was the behaviour of the Rochesters, Buckinghams, Killigrews, and, chiefest of all, that of 'the best good man that ever ruled a throne'. Licentiousness of course there was; but it was rationalized, argued, made subject to scientific tests. And if the most brilliant and amusing statement of the experiment is given in Dryden's *Marriage à la Mode*; the most profound and biting, and still more laughter-provoking in Wycherley's *Country Wife*; the most graceful in Etherege's *She Would if She Could*, in none of these cases is the result aphrodisiac. As regards licentiousness there is nothing in the whole dramatic literature of this period, not in Sedley, Otway, or Aphra Behn, that goes farther in this direction than certain scenes in *Pericles* or *Romeo and Juliet*.

It is often said that Restoration comedy was an offshoot from France, but no one who has seriously studied either French comedy or the later Elizabethan in relation to that of Charles II's time can agree that this is more than a very partial statement. French plots, it is true, were taken in abundance, but they were always transformed, doubled, reworked, so as to become, as works of art, or parts of works of art, something totally distinct. *The Plain Dealer* is as far from *Le Misanthrope* as *All's Well that Ends Well* is from Boccaccio's tale. A general influence there was, but it was linguistic rather than anything else, for the English stage has always been impatient of classical construction and economy, even when handled by such a master as Jonson. Congreve also is a classic in this respect, and he comes not from Molière but from Terence.

The chief source of Restoration comedy is the late Elizabethan—Massinger, Shirley, Brome, D'Avenant being an easy link with Cokain, Wilson, and Shadwell. Much also came from earlier sources, such as Marston; and if something in the working of intrigue came from Spain, in structure, in treatment, in the types chosen, in general movement and moral, this comedy everywhere betrays its national ancestry. Indeed, it is not altogether foolish to say that the Restoration writers completed what the Elizabethans began: that Dryden is the fitting successor of Jonson; and Rymer, with his dramatic criticism of Shakespeare, the proper descendant of Webbe with his *Arte of Poesie*. It is to be noted that in this period the centre of literary interest, the object of criticism, was not poetry, as it had been for the last hundred years, but the drama, which up to this time had undergone hardly any criticism at all. It was in many ways a timely change.

There is, of course, a difference in kind between the work of the two periods; the names Comedy of Humours and Comedy of Manners themselves indicate this; but there is no rigid dividing line, and the difference is only very obvious at the extremes. The Comedy of Manners also took types, human qualities, and worried them into all sorts of distortions, as the names Sir Fopling Flutter, Sir Positive At-All, Horner, Lady Fancyful, Mrs. Marwood are enough to show; indeed, Congreve was the one writer of his period to subtilize the 'humour' into a person. But the names, it will be noticed, are slightly different; the qualities taken are more superficial, less separated, than those of Volpone or Sir Giles Overreach. For the Restoration writers were far more realistic; they drew their characters, copied their situations, from the life they saw around them; they were much less abstract. They were concerned to bring things to earth, to test them by immediate actuality; they had none of the metaphysical background of the Elizabethans. Their comedy, therefore, is lighter, racier, more spinning; the action is brisker, the wording sharper and more epigrammatic. Their wit sometimes became wearisome, but it had its point, which was the 'acquired follies' of man, not his deep characteristics; their criticism was from a social angle, not from a humanistic one.

For Restoration comedy was, with the exception of Etherege's work, what is known as critical comedy; it tried to 'cure excess', to find the happy mean by laughing exaggeration out of court and vice out of countenance. This is in itself a limitation, for the greatest minds do not want to change anything; Shakespeare wanted to alter Falstaff about as much as Bardolph did; and if Molière held Arnolphe up to scorn, one feels he understood Tartufe to be a neces-

sary ingredient in the general make-up of the world.
It is true that Wycherley in one play, and Congreve
in another, achieved this more divine comedy, and
we need not blame the rest for not succeeding in
something they were not trying to do. Rather we
have every reason to be grateful for the restraint
which kept them making something they could make
supremely well and amusingly, for the result is a
gallery of entertaining, and partly immortal types,
involved in situations which never cease to divert
mankind. The Restoration comedy writers, with
their keen observation, their quick, even too facile,
deductions from externals, their capacity for seizing
character from a gesture, keep us dancing along to a
gay tune that is often irresistible. The fop, the idler,
the preposterous man of importance; the philanderer,
his feminine counterpart, the sham scientist, the
astrologer; the town elegant, the country cold-pole,
the seaman and the professional man; the Spanish
knot, the Chedreux wig, the fruz-toure, and the
'fanatic's' robe—all conspire to leave the busy world
and appear before us on the stage in a lively medley
of action, with robust outpouring of words.

Congreve is not wholly of the type of Restoration
dramatist; he is in some sort the descendant, rather
than the contemporary, of Etherege and Wycherley;
he is more mature. But the material he used for his
comedies hardly differs from that of his companions.
Like theirs, his people are the men and women who
talked in the boudoirs and coffee-houses of King
William's reign, and took their exercise in the Park,
the Piazza, or the Mall. They may be met in the

comedies of Crowne, Shadwell, and Dryden, in the diaries of Evelyn and Pepys, even in the letters of Dorothy Osborne. They were not very different from ourselves. Superficially their conversation seems different because the idiom has changed; we no longer rail, or hunt elusive simile to the death: but were the Petulants, the Carelesses, the Belindas, and the Brisks to appear at our own dinner-tables, we should find them natural enough. They would, with just the same zest as ourselves, use the discoveries of Dr. Freud pleasurably to widen the limits of gossip, and charitably to interpret the failings of our friends.

But part of the material an artist has at his disposal is his philosophic make-up, and here Congreve differs from his contemporaries. Not much, for his was not a profoundly original mind; he had no new orientation to declare, no revelation to make, wherewith to stir the people of his day to revision, as Signor Pirandello may have driven us lately. But he differed in two points. His intellectual fastidiousness made him loath to portray 'fools so gross, that they should rather disturb than divert the well-natured and reflecting part of an audience'; and secondly, his passionate sense rebelled against the rationalization of love. The attempt had proved a failure, and Congreve, born somewhat late in the day, could only feel the disillusion of peace, while missing the joy of battle.

But more important than the material of an artist is the use he makes of it; how else could we distinguish between Jonson and Brome, between Etherege's lace-work, and the turgid periods of

Crowne? By this is shown a writer's sensibility, his affective wealth; in this alone artistic creation makes so close the fusion of mind with sensibility, that thought merges into feeling, and we enter that realm where it really is true to say *Le style, c'est l'homme même.*

To achieve a style argues a passionate nature; it cannot be coldly constructed or artificially put together; for passion means not the noisy tearing of the heart to tatters, but the deep-rooted impulse which drives a man to labour continually in the same road. And here we hit the amazing paradox about Congreve— that not even in spite of, but actually because of his style, which almost without a gap gives evidence of exquisite feeling, he is accused of being cold, heartless, wicked. Some have seen in him nothing but a social snob, and have entered his works in the studbook as being by Pride out of Urbanity. The reason may be that, endowed with a passionate and selective nature—in this, but for fear of exaggeration, one would like to compare him with Racine—an element of physical weakness prevented its full realization either in life or in literature. Under such conditions the mind turns ever inward upon itself, continually discerning and refining, dwelling upon possibilities of human relationship, making ramifications of increasing subtlety. We see this carried to its farthest point in Proust. This would account for the strong element of wistfulness in Congreve's work, that constant fear of disillusion, that 'against fruition' note, we find so often on the lips of his women, of Cynthia, Angelica, and Millamant. Yet because

Congreve was not a sentimentalist, he applied his clear, strong mind, his discerning, if not very wide or deep imagination, to his emotions; he never deluded himself. Thus he made every effort to be dry, and his last comedy, though based on sentiment rather than on the 'humours', is far from sentimental. This is not by any means to say that it is heartless.

In discussing Congreve, then, it must be insisted that he belongs to the type of 'pure' creator, who is to be judged solely on aesthetic grounds, that is, by the quality of delight which he imparts. He and Dickens are not to be measured by the same instrument, any more than Dostoievsky and Miss Austen are, in spite of the elements they may possess in common. It is, when all is said, the province of art to delight the spirit, and it is, finally, the aesthetic pleasure we get from Congreve that earns him his high place. It is on that plane, and not on the moral or philosophic, that he has something to give.

The most evident pleasure we obtain from the drama is in the interplay of character, by the colours woven together to make up an objective view of humanity; but though in this, too, Congreve must be ranked with the masters, he does not take a very high place among them. His first piece, *The Old Bachelor*, has all the obviousness of Jonson without the especial creative purpose that made it necessary; Bluffe is a version of Bobadill, Fondlewife is modelled on Kitely; we detect patches of Brome, we scent the influence of Marston. Congreve had learned much from the old masters, but he had not yet made them his own, nor entered into the Restoration inheritance. As characterization the play adds nothing to our riches; we are still in a late Elizabethan world. In *The Double-Dealer* there is a new set of contrasts that are almost too striking, of the harsh unredeemed villains with the rightly-named Froths, and with the candid Cynthia. *Love for Love* again is a return, not to Jonson, but to the purest Wycherley. *The Way of the World*, however, soars above all, and the characterization becomes subtle and individual; too subtle almost, since even Pope was constrained to ask 'Tell me if Congreve's fools are fools indeed'. For here Congreve broke through the rules he had laid down in that happy piece of constructive criticism, the *Letter Concerning Humour in Comedy*, and made his people three-dimensional. The greatest triumph, of course, is Millamant, many-faceted, spontaneous, who hides her feeling beneath her gaiety, and is so well set off against Lady Wishfort, Mrs. Marwood, and Mrs. Fainall, not containing within herself the springs that move those others, but alive with the possibility of containing them.

Characterization, however, is not a solely dramatic element: as an ingredient it is equally important in the novel; but what we may hazard as being specifically dramatic is the changes of speed, of movement, which constitute the rhythm of a piece. You can have 'great still novels' like those of Richardson, you cannot have a play that those adjectives will suit. It may even be said that a dramatic moment is definitely

that where the rhythm changes, of which the knock-
ing at the gate in *Macbeth* may be taken as one *locus
classicus*, and Cleopatra's 'Peace! Peace! Dost thou
not see my baby at my breast That sucks the nurse
asleep?' as another, in the reverse direction. For, as
in physical life, it is not motion that we feel, but
change of motion. In the drama this varying of speed
may be achieved by the introduction of new persons,
by changes of tempo, or by the quality of the phrasing,
this last consciously and most superbly done by
Jonson in *Catiline*. Of all these methods Congreve
was a master, producing results of delicious beauty.
When his works were reprinted, he made the
addition or loss of a person upon the stage constitute
a new scene, not to borrow a French habit, but to
emphasize the change of tempo, and to allow each
scene to be itself a separate jewel. To give only one
example of how, by phrasing alone, he could alter
the speed, it will be enough to point out the stagger-
ing finale of *The Double-Dealer*. The play has been
proceeding at a glorious and ever-increasing pace;
until the last moment we are borne along in a
tremendous rush; it seems incredible that the curtain
should not come down upon a tumult: but then:

Brisk. This is all very surprising, let me perish!
Lady Froth. You know I told you Saturn looked a little
more angry than usual.

This shows his strength: we are suddenly pulled
up sharp. A technically similar, but in tone vastly
different, ending to *The Way of the World* illustrates
his grace, like that of a pigeon, which hurtling

through the air with closed wings, opens them to alight on the selected branch. It is all done by phrasing; for it is in prose that Congreve most surely excels.

Dryden's panegyric, contained in the lines that preface *The Double-Dealer*, was no affected piece of homage such as grey hairs sometimes pay to gold. For the hoary monarch of Will's had, in a famous phrase, found the language brick and left it marble, and he saw in Congreve a young man working unerringly in the new medium. Here, at last, was a poet 'lineal to the throne', an artist who realized that his material was words, who loved words, glorying in their proper and beautiful use. He could not but admire a boy who began a first comedy with:

Vainlove, and abroad so early! good morrow; I thought a contemplative lover could no more have parted with his bed in a morning, than he could have slept in't.

He immediately rejoiced in the amazing skill, so surely shown, in the difficult matter of spacing stresses.

To any one who has not thought about stage dialogue the speech may not seem very striking; yet it is a sound piece of craftsmanship. For stage prose, like pulpit, or even law-court prose, is not to be judged in the same way as chamber prose, or that written for the inward ear. Browne so enthralling to murmur to oneself; Swift so delightful to read to one's friend; Gibbon so effective and amusing to quote, would empty box and gallery alike; while the grandiose periods of Burke sent the Mother of Parliaments to dinner. For stage prose must be easy to say at once rapidly and loud; it must suit the human lungs working under specialized conditions. The weight must always be brought naturally, and rather obviously, on to the important word. That is why, if we compare a passage from *The Silent Woman* with one of Jonson's dedications, or a description of a masque, we find the prose so markedly different; and why, if we put a speech from *Marriage à la Mode* against an extract from the *Essay of Dramatick Poesy* we get the same variance. That Congreve understood how the rhythm of stage writing had to differ from the balance of other forms can be proved in a moment by any one who cares, however cursorily, to turn over the pages of his books.

But in his first play, for prose as well as for persons, Congreve chose Jonson for his master. If we take a typical piece of the latter's work, we can see that the same kind of beat runs through *The Old Bachelor*:

Yes, faith. The fellow trims him silently, and has not the knack with his shears or his fingers: and that continency in a barber he thinks so eminent a virtue, as it has made him chief of his counsel (*The Silent Woman*, I. 2).

For Congreve's lighter touch, however, Jonson was too fond of accented syllables; and his prose, though rarely blank verse, in beat-structure resembles his own to an extraordinary degree. Moreover, he was inclined to come down too heavily on the last syllable:

If she be short, let her sit much, lest when she stands, she be thought to sit, &c. (*The Silent Woman*, IV. I).

and this sometimes gives his work a kind of gaunt, hammered stiffness, admirable for what he was trying to do, but lacking in the lilt Congreve required for differently felt persons. He wanted something more fluid, and perhaps he applied to Dryden:

You speak more truly than you think: I have shown it. For, since I must confess the truth to you, I am no fortune: my father, tho' he bears it high, to put me off, has mortgaged his estate. We keep servants for show, and when we should pay their wages, pick a quarrel with their service, and turn 'em off penniless (*Love Triumphant*, IV).

That is a fair average sample of Dryden's stage prose; it is charming enough to the inward ear, but is not of quite the first class for stage enunciation. In his prose plays Dryden never seemed quite sure of his rhythm, and, perhaps through fear of slipping into the 'other harmony' of verse, often ran too many unstressed syllables together. He here lacked the splendid assurance of his critical and controversial essays, as much as he did the irrestible march of his verse. But Congreve learned something of flexibility from him, and how to deal with runs; as he learned, it may be, a certain swing from Etherege, and how to introduce the note of lyrical sadness into comedy:

Did you not tell me there was no credit to be given to faces? That women nowadays have their passions as much at will as they have their complexions, and put on joy and sadness, scorn and kindness, with the same ease as they do their paint and patches.—Are they the only counterfeits? (*The Man of Mode*, v. 2).

Etherege more nearly approaches Congreve for a sensitive ear than any other dramatist of the period, but he had not the rich polyphonic mastery of vowels; while Wycherley, giant as he was, something neglected his surface in the bigger scale of his conceptions.[1]

But to have done with Congreve's predecessors, and to come to his own progress. The attentive reader will, I think, see that in *The Old Bachelor* he definitely tried to soften the angles of his model:

> Lard I have seen an ass look so chagrin, ha! ha! ha! (you must pardon me I can't help laughing) that an absolute lover would have concluded the poor creature to have had darts, and flames, and altars, and all that in his breast (II. 3),

a passage in which he veered away from Jonson to write nearly pure Dryden. Again, he did not always avoid the pitfall gaping for those who wish to write swift, rhetorical prose, and occasionally fell into blank verse:

> Methinks I feel the woman strong within me,
> And vengeance kindles in the room of love (III. 1).

His measure, too, sometimes missed the right balance of prose to hit upon that of poetry:

> and called him aloud in your sleep (II. 3)

reminding one over-forcibly of such metres as:

> And left him alone in his glory.

But his next play shows an enormous advance:

> My mind gives me it won't—because we are both willing; we each of us strive to reach the goal, and hinder one another in the race; I swear it never does well when the parties are so agreed.—For when people walk hand in hand, there's neither

---

[1] The curious may like to trace Congreve's descent from Cowley. It is an opinion I would maintain after dinner, supported by *Cutter of Coleman Street*, IV. 5, 6, but for which I would not go to the stake.

overtaking nor meeting. We hunt in couples where we both pursue the same game, but forget one another; and 'tis because we are so near that we don't think of coming together (*The Double-Dealer*, IV. 1).

Here he achieved a larger rhythmical unit than was common with Jonson, but yet preserved an admirable stress spacing; and in the second part of the paragraph varied the phrase endings to contrast beautifully with those in the first. He was more aware, too, of the value of vowel changes. *Goal* with *race* is effective; and if *agreed* and *meeting* constitute an experiment that does not quite come off, we shall see later what he could do, in the plenitude of his power, by playing on the same sound.

Love for Love was an attempt to re-create *The Plain Dealer's* scenes of Manly rage; but whosoever would lash the follies of the time is compelled to use a certain medium, and some of the earlier passages of this play are pure Wycherley. Congreve's rhythm, however, was vastly superior once he plunged into his own atmosphere:

What a bustle did you keep against the last invisible eclipse, laying in provision as 'twere for a siege? What a world of fire and candle, matches and tinderboxes did you purchase! One would have thought we were ever after to live under ground, or at least making a voyage to Greenland, to inhabit there all the dark season (II. 3).

In this play, too, the listening reader will find a blank verse couplet (IV. 19) as he may have noticed some in *The Double-Dealer* (e.g. V. 13), but it is in *Love for Love* that we really begin to hear the melody that pervades *The Way of the World*—that melody which was most readily Congreve's in the tenderer passages, for instance in the one which begins 'You're a woman—one to whom Heaven gave beauty, when it grafted roses on a briar' (iv. 16), or that wonderful paragraph 'Would any thing but a madman complain of uncertainty' (iv. 20), much of which *could* be twisted into blank verse, and which perhaps gains its effect because it does all the time seem to skim perilously along the brink.

The Way of the World is throughout authentic Congreve, and is of incomparable beauty in its kind. Here, whatever he may have learned from his predecessors, he made something peculiarly his own, impossible to imitate. For sinewy flexibility and point, combined with seductive gentleness; for the full gamut of vowel sounds and the varied spacing of stresses, English literature had to wait for Landor until it once more heard a voice that had something of the especial quality of Congreve. Addison, for instance, made far too flat a country out of Congreve's beautifully accidented landscape, and one has only to read *The Drummer* to see how short he fell.

For his satiric passages Congreve could still use the Jonsonian regular ring, coming down thump on the last syllable with a spondee; or 'keen iambics, i'Gad', like locking the door upon a prisoner:

For a fool's visit is always a disguise; and never admitted by a woman of wit, but to blind her affair with a lover of sense (iii. 10).

But when he came to the more delicate passages, especially when he wished to move to sympathy, he nearly always closed upon a trochee, with that plaintive, almost melancholy effect Landor used so well, and that Fletcher tried to get with the feminine double-ending in blank verse. In the same way he transformed down the rather too marked contrasts in the vowel sounds in the antithetical parts of the sentence, the broad distinction having become too common a trick, and wearisome in the writings of such as Halifax. Take even that torrential passage at the beginning of the last act, wherein Lady Wishfort is not only 'at once concise and voluble', but a poetess:

> Out of my house, out of my house, thou viper, thou serpent, that I have fostered; thou bosom traitress, that I have raised from nothing—begone, begone, begone, go, go—that I took from washing of old gauze and weaving of dead hair, with a bleak blue nose, over a chafing-dish of starved embers, and dining behind a traverse-rag, in a shop no bigger than a bird-cage,—go, go, starve again, do, do.

Facit indignatio versum! and it was certainly no ordinary inspiration that imagined that splendidly incisive 'bleak blue nose', with its deepening sound to clinch the delicious modelling of 'from washing of old gauze and weaving of dead hair'; or fathered the equally effective change from 'traverse-rag' to 'bird-cage', and the final return to 'starve'.

If one were to have to select the two lines that best exhibit Congreve's flavour, one might do worse than choose the sentence that ushers in Millamant for the first time:

> Here she comes i' faith full sail, with her fan spread and streamers out, and a shoal of fools for tenders—Ha, no, I cry her mercy (II. 4).

The beauty of that needs no insistence; the delicate play of the vowels, the dancing rhythm, with the sharp uptake at the end attended with the entirely new sound of 'cry', sweep us away with their effect of spontaneity. And see, too, a little later in the same scene, how skilfully he can now play on one note, recurring to the same word:

Beauty the lover's gift—Lord, what is a lover that it can give? Why one makes lovers as fast as one pleases, and they live as long as one pleases, and they die as soon as one pleases: and then, if one pleases, one makes more.

'How it chimes, and cries tink in the close, divinely!' The reiteration never gives the ear the smallest bother, because, said as they must be to gain the full meaning, the phrases only gather their weight upon 'pleases' in the last instance, the stresses otherwise playing all around it. At last the voice fatefully pounces upon the word, as a hawk, after several feints, lands upon a predestined prey.

Those extracts are from that miraculous second act, which shows a more consummate mastery than any other passage in the dramatic literature of the period. The whole rhythm of changes of swiftness from scene to scene is astoundingly beautiful and moving. The pace is made up of varying emotions, from the corrosive jealousy of Mrs. Marwood to the almost too sweet melancholy of Mirabell, and in every instance the phrasing is perfectly adapted, as well to the highest gaiety as to the gravest doubt. Nor are we at any time kept too long at the same pitch, and the succeeding scene always seems just the right one to modulate the change of our emotions. In its tuneful measure the passage between the lovers reminds one of the second act of *Le Tartuffe*; and there the whole of Millamant is revealed, the wise and winning woman who knows that life is so serious that we cannot afford always to be serious about it, and wear for ever an inflexible wise face.

Yet it is not surprising that the play failed at first performance, for it does in truth 'evaporate into an essence almost too fine', and one cannot but suspect that Congreve was writing for himself alone, forgetting a little the cruder exigencies of the stage. Whence it may be said of *The Way of the World* what is often remarked of Shakespeare's plays, that it is better in the study than on the scene. With neither is this absurdity true; all it means is that intimacy of reading discloses beauties that cannot immediately be snatched, and that thoroughly to enjoy these plays in the acting we must first of all know them well. Then one awaits the delicious phrase, the thrilling movement, the breath-catching swerve of tempo, even as one expects the enunciation of a theme in a familiar Bach concerto, or revels in the arabesque of a well-known page of counterpoint. And this, perhaps, is a touchstone for the surest works of art, only to reveal their final perfection to the lover; for though, to be commended, an aspirant must declare some grace, in its most treasured, its most enriching forms, beauty is the lover's gift indeed.

V

RICHARD STEELE

THE persuasiveness, combined with the pontifical certainty, of Macaulay's prose has often done more to fix the character and value of writers he treated than the actual works and deeds of the men themselves. His sentences come with such a ring of robust veracity that we are apt not to notice that he is so often wrong. Thus his opinion of Steele, in spite of what Forster and Thackeray could do to annul the effect, still largely holds the field. 'He was one of those people', we are assured, 'whom it is impossible either to hate or to respect. His temper was sweet, his affections warm, his spirits lively, and his principles weak . . .' and so on, even to accusing him of being a swindler. It is true that he had not such punctuality in paying his debts as to make him a pillar of honour in a commercial society, but he never swindled anybody but himself; and if his principles were weak, the passions which rode them must have been rarely well directed; for they carried him into trouble and distress, through the support of doctrines not shared by the great, in a manner which has all the air of durable determination. It is his crime that he 'sought the public weal, but not his own'; whereas his more discreet and sagacious friends managed to combine the two so as to bring them profit as well as renown.

The single grudge that we feel against him is that he should have been so self-abasing; his itch to con-

fess is a trifle exaggerated; his humility seems a
perversion of his riotous generosity: it would be
mean to appear more virtuous than one's friends.
Yet it is his faculty for wearing his heart upon his
sleeve, as a true creature of impulse, that makes him
so vivid a figure to-day. He knew, of course, that if
his instincts were not always of the most respectable
they were shared by most healthy men. It was no
doubt his careless dash, his spontaneity, which made
him attractive to Addison, just as it may have been
Addison's somewhat chilly self-control which caused
Steele to admire him. He was optimistic in the
extreme, almost gullible, involving himself in later
years in the wild 'fish-pools' scheme of bringing
salmon alive to London, just as in his earlier days he
had dabbled in alchemy: he even thought he could
reconcile warring Churches. If he could live gaily,
as well as live hard, there is this of peculiar about
him—that though he liked to be popular, though he
loved the good opinion of his friends and basked in
the praise of his wife, he always went his own way.
He was sometimes ridiculous; but, as Stevenson
remarked, 'God help the man who is afraid of making
a fool of himself!' He was, no doubt, in a strict view,
a little sentimental—that is, he felt his emotional
experiences more than is consistent with a wholesome
balance; but it is largely this capacity for acute feeling
that gave him the sympathy which makes him the
first of our intimate essayists. He never forgot the
hideous experience of nearly killing his man in a
duel, so never ceased to inveigh against duelling: he
always remembered the distresses of fathering a

natural child, so always insisted upon the difference between love and lust. He could not have seen the higher had he not pursued the lower, but he need not have insisted so much on his falls from grace. It was that which enabled Macaulay to refer to him sneeringly as spending a life 'in sinning and repenting, in inculcating what was right, and doing what was wrong'. It may be true that it is the fool who learns only from his own experience, but the wisdom which grows from the experience of others is shallow and disagreeable. Better to err with Steele than shine in rectitude with Addison.

To belittle Addison is the rock every writer on Steele must seek to avoid; yet it is almost impossible. He can only sigh with Hazlitt, 'I am far from wishing to depreciate Addison's talents, but I am anxious to do justice to Steele'. That we cannot do the latter without now and then drifting upon the former is to some extent Steele's own fault, as he himself realized with some bitterness after Addison's death, when Tickell, Addison's literary executor, went to show that Steele had sought to build up his reputation on Addison's writings. The truth was that Steele had been 'very patiently traduced and calumniated for' certain papers Addison had not wished to own. Indeed it was his wholesale and admiring acknowledgement to Addison in the preface to the *Tatler* which caused generations to give him less than was fair. He would not mind; he sought his friend's weal much more than his own; and even at the end it was his bountiful heart which made him rush in to the attack of the meddlesome Tickell. It is the result of his own selflessness that, like his Sir Roger, he has been 'rather loved than esteemed'; a happy state of affairs, perhaps, which Steele would have welcomed; but the critic who attempts to estimate him two hundred years after his death must strive to give him his due.

Here we are on healthier ground, for though the writings of the two men are sometimes so alike as to make it hard to distinguish between them, there are certain qualities to be rendered to Steele and others to Addison. On the whole, the originality is Steele's: it was he who began the *Tatler* without saying a word to Addison about it, so it was he who conceived the plan, the drawing in of a certain number of 'characters', just as it was he who later sketched in Sir Roger de Coverley and his group. His was the idea to civilize London life in a way different from, more humane and more effective than, that of the Society for the Reformation of Manners, as well as that of the tactful method of the dangerous procedure. The first letters, anecdotes and allegories are his. It is often forgotten that out of the 271 *Tatlers*, 188 are by Steele, only forty-two by Addison, while thirty-six are by them both. The *Tatler* improved as it progressed, partly through Steele's widening experience, but partly, no doubt whatever, because of Addison's help and stimulation; in the *Spectator* it was Addison who took the lion's share. The fact is that both throve in collaboration. Addison's papers are certainly more polished, perhaps because he had more leisure, but more likely because he was the finer craftsman. Certainly the mind at work is no

better, but the erudition is greater, the finish more
perfect; the most delicious literary toys are from his
pen. Yet in some ways Steele's papers are more
delightful—we are here with Hazlitt and Landor—
because they are more friendly, less removed; there
is more of the street and the open air in them. With
Addison the gusto is too refined down; it all smells
a little of the study, whereas we feel that Steele's
things were written in the coffee-house as a direct
reaction to life. We have a sense of this also in their
prose; there is more nerve and vivacity in Steele's,
while Addison's is a little dulcet, the movement
something too slow and urbane. There is rather
much of the looker-on in Addison; indeed (he need
not have confined his statement to parties) he never
espoused anything with violence.

Though the end at which both men aimed was the
same—namely, to make mankind better, wiser, and
therefore happier—the motives were different. Steele
was urged by a 'great benevolence', Addison by an
abstract love of virtue. The difference between the
two men, in attitude and in prose style, is beautifully
illustrated by their statements as to the impulses
which made them write. Thus Steele in the last *Tatler*:

I must confess it has been a most exquisite pleasure to me
to frame characters of domestic life, and put those parts of it
which are least observed into an agreeable view; to inquire
into the seeds of vanity and affection, to lay before the readers
the emptiness of ambition: in a word, to trace human life
through all its mazes and recesses, and show much shorter
methods than men ordinarily practise to be happy, agreeable
and great.

And thus Addison, in a famous passage of the tenth *Spectator*:

It was said of Socrates that he brought philosophy down from heaven, to inhabit among men; and I shall be ambitious to have it said of me, that I have brought philosophy out of closets and libraries, schools and colleges, to dwell in clubs and assemblies, at tea-tables and in coffee-houses.

It is the joy of doing as opposed to the ambition for praise; the thing for its own sake rather than for the result; the delight in life as it is, as against the pleasure of life as it ought to be: on the one hand, vitality ending on a firm note; on the other, the drawing-room manner slowing down to a trochee.

Steele's genius is most apparent in his bold launching out into the new venture of journalistic literature, in his conception both of the form it was to take and of the audience it was to appeal to. In form, the nearest approach so far had been Defoe's admirable *Review*, which was too polemical; while cognate descriptive writing of the time, such as Ned Ward's the *London Spy* or *The Amusements Serious and Comical* of Tom Brown, 'of facetious memory,' were far too heavy to provide breakfast-table fare. Essayists also there had been, but of the more studious variety, such as Cowley and Temple; while the philosophic writers, Shaftesbury for instance, wrote that sterner stuff which it is the province rather of philosophers than of the town to read. Well-timed, above all, was the revival of the 'character', a form practised by many in this country—Sir Thomas Overbury, Samuel Butler—though his were not

published till much later—and others, most notably
John Earle, who in *Microcosmography* reveals much
of the gentle humour, the general kindliness, which
is the mark of Steele's, and, to a lesser degree since
a certain pointed and agreeable malice creeps in, of
Addison's. La Bruyère also had his influence. But
it was the combination of these elements into a whole,
which would be delectable to the audience which
Steele sought to attract, that led to the immediate
success of the *Tatler*.

A deal has been made of the appeal to the 'fair
sex'; but the emergence of reading women cannot
be separated from the change which was coming over
society, a society which the theatre was beginning
to attract, but for which most other writing, apart
from more or less scurrilous romances, was far too
abstract and literary. It was the rise of a middle class
with enough education to wish to read, and enough
leisure to gratify the wish, which made up the new
audience ready to be captured by such a journal, an
audience larger than the comparatively small class
of University men and their families. Thus Mr. Sea-
land in *The Conscious Lovers* remarks:

> I know the town and the world; and give me leave to say
> that we merchants are a species of gentry that have grown
> into the world this last century, and are as honourable, and
> almost as useful, as you landed folks, that have always thought
> yourselves so much above us.

He knew the town and the world, and he wanted
literature which dealt with the town and the world
that he knew; his wife and daughters would also

want it, for most did not have the chance of being the good type of gentlewoman, with her especial responsibilities, and did not on the whole want to imitate the bad type, with her routs and masquerades, her quadrille, her chair and her patches—in short, all the dull frivolity of mode.

Since it was to this large new class that the paper was to appeal, it was to be light and amusing: it would rely upon the middle-class prejudice against the fashionable world and would glorify trade. Above all, it would be moral, for when a class rises to power it is always upon its superior morality that it insists as a justification for its search after position. The morality and the conventions, therefore, were commonplace enough—what oft was thought but hardly ever expressed, at least in popular writing: there could hardly be any of the upsetting notions of that forerunner of Nietzsche, Bernard Mandeville. Addison wished to make it serve also to cool the heats of faction; but, though Steele might have desired this, his passions were too strong to permit him to remain permanently out of the political turmoil. It was no use Addison being 'in a thousand troubles for poor Dick'; he could only stand on the bank ready to pull him out of the current whenever he was in risk of drowning; he could not prevent him from plunging into the stream. When Whig principles were at stake he would infallibly embroil himself. It was this sad propensity which led to the abrupt termination of the *Tatler*, to Steele's non-participation in the last volume of the *Spectator*, his writing of the *Englishman* and the fatal *Crisis*, and eventually the *Plebeian*, which brought about his final rupture with Addison.

Yet if it was not the 'fair sex' apart from its males which determined the form of the paper, it is obvious that the improvement of the position of women was one of its real objects, for Steele realized that it is women who determine the niceties of civilization. And since it was clear that they were to play an important part in society, it was necessary that they should become more serious, more enlightened—in a word, emancipated. Steele had a livelier sympathy for women than Addison had, and Thackeray was right to make Esmond say, 'There's not a writer of my time of any note, with the exception of poor Dick Steele, that does not speak of a woman as of a slave, and scorn and use her as such.' But here it was not altogether Steele's 'benevolence' that was at work; it was his Bohemian nature. He had, certainly, no use for the intelligent—but not too intelligent—household drudge, which was Addison's ideal; true, he did not want women to be wasteful, silly, and vain; but then, dreadful alternative, they might develop into household autocrats. The problem was, and perhaps still is, not how women may be happiest, but how men may be happiest with women. If it was bad to be married to a foolish dependent little creature, it was even worse to be held in leash by a would-be ruler. Thus in Steele's first comedy, written as early as 1701, Lord Hardy declares that he expects his felicity from his wife 'in her friendship, her constancy, her piety, her household cares, her maternal tenderness'. Friendship comes first; and it led to the question which crops up in the periodicals, 'Can a wife be to her husband as a friend?' The answer was 'Yes'; but it was born of Steele's hopes rather than of his experience.

Of his first short-lived marriage there is little to be said; and soon after his first wife's death he married Mary Scurlock, to whom he was passionately devoted. Nevertheless, he began to find that, as well as being his 'dear Prue', she was also his 'dear ruler' and his 'peevish beauty'. Certainly she had much to suffer, a little because her husband might end a note to her, 'I am, dear Prue, a little in drink, but at all times your faithful husband'; yet his intemperance, which was not so outrageous as his detractors make out, was the smallest of her worries. The worst was that she never knew whether they were rich or poor, whether she could afford another dress or run up a butcher's bill; and she knew that no patrimony for the children was being put by. For in all Steele's schemes for educating women to be their husbands' friends he forgot that if this were to come about a wife would have to be as financially independent of her husband as his friends were. All Steele considered was that a friend left you alone; he did not question your goings out and your comings in, nor make a fuss if you failed to turn up to dinner or arrived home 'a little in drink'.

The point is worth labouring a little, since much has been made of Steele as a liberator of women, and it is as well to see exactly where he stands. It is not that he had no ideal for women, an ideal they could cultivate for their own sakes. He is responsible for the delightful character of Aspasia, often attributed

to Congreve, and in another essay struck out the
famous phrase, 'Though her mien carries much
more invitation than command, to behold her is an
immediate check to loose behaviour, and to love her
is a liberal education'. But he felt that if only a
woman had enough to keep her mind full, she would
not bother about her husband's doings: there was
the advantage. Prue was always fretting, and Steele
would constantly have to send her little notes to
explain that he could not come home punctually, to
state whom he was with, and why. Loving her as
he did, he made every effort to treat her peppery
objections as signs of her devotion: 'Your letter
shows you are passionately in love with me,' he would
reply to a scolding. But she must leave him alone.
'I have not rebelled against you but all the rest of my
governors,' he once declared; and it was true, for he
had always gone his own way since the day he for-
feited an estate in Ireland for leaving Oxford to ride
privately in the guards. But she would not learn;
and it was annoying to have to add to a note saying
he was supping with Mr. Boyle, 'Dear Prue, don't
send after me, for I shall be ridiculous'. It was
absurd that his intercourse with his oldest and best
friend should irk her, so that he was able to refer to
Addison as 'your rival'. He had to tell her that, 'To
attend to my business as I ought, and improve my
fortune, it is necessary that my time and my will
should be under no direction but my own'. A wife
should not be a 'sovereign director'. She was to be
a friend, who would converse with him and go about
with him, confine her domestic cares to her own

spheres, the kitchen and the nursery, and leave him
to his own combats.

Later on, when in desperation to get something
straight, and perhaps also because Steele was too
warm a lover, she retired for over a year to Wales,
we still find him urging his wife to enjoy herself, be
his companion, and to cease worrying. A woman
should be independent-minded enough to rise above
trifles, and converse intelligently: 'to look well, a
woman must think well'.

But Steele was not really consistent; a man makes
certain intimate demands upon his wife, from which
a friend is free; but if she is to be independent she
has a right to refuse them, a course Lady Steele took
until such time as her spendthrift husband should
settle her securely and make provision for the children. Steele had no right to grumble, and object that
he was forced to wean himself from habits he had
grown accustomed to. It was his sentimentality
which really was to blame; he thought that protesta-
tions of love—which he sincerely felt—flattery,
cajolery, calling her his 'governess' and himself her
'obsequious servant', and being as extremely fond of
the children as his charming letters show, would
serve instead of paying bills. As he himself admitted,
he could always get money; the difficulty was to
keep it.

For though for the last twenty-five years of his
extremely active and bustling life his emoluments
and takings, from his post as gazetteer, stamp commissioner, theatre licensee, Scottish commissioner,
and so on, from his *Tatlers*, *Guardians*, pamphlets,

and plays, had been considerable, actions against him
for debt scarcely ever failed to mark a term. He would
not bother about money until he was forced to. He
lived his turbulent and contentious life to the top
of his bent, and revelled in political squabbles as
much as in a convivial evening rich in talk and wine.
Some found it possible to hate him, more to respect
him, but most to love him; and when, three years
before his death, he retired to Wales, there were
many who regretted no longer seeing about the town
the burly figure, surmounted by the swarthy face
and the brilliant eyes, which they had known as
Dicky, or Captain, or Sir Richard Steele. He left
his mark upon his generation, not by his plays, for
these, drawn largely from Corneille, Molière, and
Terence, have the broad vivacity of Vanbrugh and
the irony of Farquhar only in a lesser degree, but by
the personality operant in his papers.

It is incredible to conceive the effect his writings have had
on the town [Gay wrote in 'The Present State of Wit'];
how many thousand follies they have either quite banished,
or given a very great check to . . . his writings have set all our
wits and men of letters upon a new way of thinking . . . we
may venture to affirm that every one of them writes and thinks
much more justly than they did some time since.

This is perhaps to rate the effect of one man too high.
Steele, brilliant journalist that he was, sensed what
was in the air—reform of manners, the education of
women, the change in the drama—and led the public
the way its best elements wanted to go. He was
himself of its very best elements. There is no need
to pity 'poor Dick'; he died, as he had lived, with an

aura of good nature and sympathy around him; and
if he attained to no great position, largely owing to
his reckless honesty, there are few who can have
enjoyed life so fully and yet left an enduring monu-
ment behind them.

VI

MANDEVILLE'S FABLE OF THE BEES

THE history of scepticism is a long and honourable
one. Man, in his continual struggle to make
himself as different as possible from the animals, or
at any rate to see himself as such, began at a very
early stage to endue himself with affections and
faculties too near the divine to be healthy for him;
he soon needed the salutary salt dose of the sceptic
to restore him to proportion. But doses are nasty,
the giver of them apt to be unpopular. Taken in
too generous quantities they may be dangerous, and
the well-wishing doctors have often been regarded
as little better than murderers. And on the whole,
scepticism, though it may be welcome to moral
idlers, your 'since we know nothing, what does it
matter what we do?' dilettantes, to most it means the
swallowing of unpalatable truths, an earthquake-
shifting of assumptions, a discovery that we are not
so good, so beautiful, and so true as we thought we
were. Is it possible that this or that prized virtue
of ours is really only sinful, or at best, weak self-
indulgence? 'Thus thousands give money to beggars
from the same motive as they pay their corn-cutters,
to walk easy': that is Mandeville. 'Ce qu'on nomme
libéralité n'est le plus souvent que la vanité de
donner': that is La Rochefoucauld. Quotations might
be multiplied by the score, for they make an un-
comfortably large crowd, these sceptics; not all of
them ungenial, however: there was Montaigne.

But an axe still more savage than that which bursts open the raree-box of motive is to the sceptics' hand; the first is a mere, if indecent, Paul-Prying sort of fellow compared with this second one, which is to be laid to the roots not only of our self-esteem, but of our existence as thinking beings. Are not animals simply automata, as Gassendi held; and is not man simply a kind of animal, equally automatic, as the Behaviourists think to-day? And the more we know, the less things turn out to be what they seem. Lucretius pointed out that a flock of sheep on a distant hill-side looks like a solid mass, though made up of little parts: Berkeley went still further, and proved that nothing was what it seemed. But Berkeley, having differentiated, to use a mathematical term, proceeded to his solution by taking the next step, and integrating:

You see, Hylas, Philonous says, the water of yonder fountain, how it is forced upwards, in a round column, to a certain height, at which it breaks, and falls back into the basin from whence it rose: its ascent as well as descent proceeding from the same uniform law or principle of *gravitation*. Just so, the same principles which, at first view, lead to Scepticism, pursued to a certain point, bring men back to common sense.

Common sense, however, for the good Bishop of Cloyne meant Christianity: for Mandeville it meant that though Christianity was very fine *in vacuo*, and that everything contrary to it was vice, it was so exalted as to be hopelessly beyond the reach of poor human kind, if not totally contrary to the very things by which men lived in anything but the most primitive state. You couldn't blunt his axes that way:

his chief one was the first, but he would use the second when he wished.

Bernard Mandeville (for he dropped the *de*) was a Dutchman, born in 1670, who in due course studied philosophy and medicine at Leyden, and in 1691 emerged as a doctor who specialized, as his father had done, in what we would call nervous diseases and affections of the stomach, but which in those days were called the 'hypochondriack and hysterick passions'. He then toured Europe, concluding in England to learn the language; but much liking this country, he settled down in it, and in 1699 married an Englishwoman. There are advantages in being cosmopolitan, and Mandeville enjoyed them to the full: if it was easy and natural for him to read Locke, he was brought up under the influence of Spinoza: if, as a good Englishman, he pondered over Hobbes, yet Montaigne and Bayle presented no difficulties. And, moreover, if you are cosmopolitan, you are tied to no tradition; you are not double-dyed in the same prejudices as the people among whom you live; it is possible to be detached without making any very great effort, or doing violence to your upbringing. You may even permit yourself to be paradoxical.

Little is known of Mandeville's life, except that he practised his craft, apparently with some success, working occasionally with Sir Hans Sloane, and attending the Earl of Macclesfield, Lord Chancellor. His geniality as a physician made him a friend of Macclesfield's; and indeed, in that well-living age, when, according to Addison, a man who lived 'suit-

able to his quality' could not avoid being fat, his
general views on diet should have made him popular.
The Lord Chancellor would sometimes interrupt
the good physician's zestful degustations by asking,
'Is this ragout wholesome, Dr. Mandeville? May I
venture to taste this stewed carp?' 'Does it agree
with your Lordship, and do you like it?' 'Yes.'
'Then eat moderately, and it must be wholesome.'
Yet allied with this, and partly due to a humanitarian
feeling (he wrote a most moving account of a
slaughtered ox), he had leanings towards vegetarian-
ism. Was meat, which had to be cooked before it
was digestible, suitable food for human beings? The
lion, now, 'has a ferment within him that consumes
the toughest skins, and hardest bones'. The lion
might devour meat with impunity. Yet, evidently,
Mandeville was none of your doctors whose joy is to be
moral as well as bodily healers, and who, with ill-con-
cealed delight, condemn you to a penitentiary table.

Yet in spite of this his practice was not large, if we
can judge from certain passages in his works which
seem to be autobiographical. 'I could never go
through a multiplicity of business . . . I am naturally
slow, and could no more attend a dozen patients in a
day, and think of them as I should do, than I could fly.'
He was not among the physicians of *The Grumbling
Hive* (in a passage to which Coleridge, together with
that on lawyers, gave 'fine Hudibrastic vigour') who

valu'd Fame and Wealth

Above the drooping Patients' Health

Or their own Skill:

for he wanted to take his time to think, which indeed,

in the treatment of hysterick and hypochondriack disorders, is essential. And besides, though he 'hated a crowd', he was 'a great lover of company'. Benjamin Franklin was in 1725 'carried to a pale-alehouse in Cheapside', where Mandeville, he recorded, had a club, 'of which he was the soul, being a most facetious, entertaining companion'. Above all, he wanted leisure to enjoy his thoughts about the people he met. 'Not that I love to be idle; but I want to be employed to my own liking.' And the employment he most liked was psychology, an examination into people's motives, and 'in private, he never ceased from examining into himself'. Having come to certain conclusions, he found he enjoyed life; and this very relish of life, he declared, 'was accompanied with an elevation of mind that seemed to be inseparable from his being'. If he highly appreciated Lord Macclesfield's port, his chief delight was in thinking, in analysing humanity, and, with humanity, himself. In a phrase, the ideal life which he proposed to himself, and successfully carried out, was that of high living and plain thinking. If he had a fault, it was that he was too much given to parson-baiting.

The temptation was too strong, because, to his thinking, all Christians were, well, to put it bluntly, liars: they mistook their own motives. Acts might seem virtuous, but the foundation of virtue was quite other from what the virtuous supposed; in fact, true virtue did not exist. 'Nos vertus ne sont le plus souvent que des vices déguisés'—that is La Rochefoucauld again. Mandeville declared roundly that 'The more we search into human nature, the more we shall be convinced that the moral virtues are the political offspring which flattery begot upon pride'. There is nothing really so shocking in all this, certainly nothing anti-social, if we take into account what Mandeville meant by virtue. He adopted, with a certain impish glee, the extreme 'rigoristic' attitude, which took the line that no action was virtuous which contained the least alloy of 'passion', for then it was merely self-gratification. Thus, though he did not deny the existence of compassion, expending indeed several pages upon it, from being himself compassionate (though, like Nietzsche, he regarded pity as the weak man's emotion), he claimed that actions which sprang from it were no virtue, since to relieve the feeling was agreeable. 'He had a strong aversion to rigorists of all sorts', we gather, so he loved making fools of them. If all men were virtuous, he argued, the state would crumble: if all men were honest, frugal, entirely self-controlled, the nation would soon be bankrupt. The moral of *The Grumbling Hive, Or Knaves turn'd Honest*, is that 'vice' is essential to civilized living, and that it is absurd to grumble at it:

> Then leave complaints: Fools only strive
> To make a Great an Honest Hive. . . .
> Bare Virtue can't make Nations live
> In Splendor; they that would revive
> A Golden Age, must be as free
> For Acorns, as for Honesty,

a doctrine which laid him open to attack. But his opponents neglected to observe the couplet:

> So Vice is beneficial found
> When it's by Justice lopt and bound:

P

and, as a reasonable man, he stated clearly where the line was to be drawn. 'When I assert that vices are inseparable from great and potent societies, and that it is impossible that wealth and grandeur should subsist without, I do not say that the particular members of them who are guilty of any should not be continually reproved, or not punished for them when they grow into crimes.'

Good, then, comes out of evil: but Mandeville's view was not the optimistic one of the school of philosophy which discovers that because that is so, therefore whatever is, is right, the universe perfect. Pope, in Mandeville's day, was the great popular exponent of the view, but Dryden had expressed it as well:

> Whatever is, is in its causes just;
> Since all things are by Fate. But purblind man
> Sees but a part o' th' chain; the nearest links;
> His eyes not carrying to that equal beam
> That poises all above.

For our sage analyst, whatever good may arise from vices, they were vices still.

Of course Mandeville, really, is all the time making fun of the rigoristic school, to which he pays lip service; and indeed the fun is easy enough to make: for if the only virtuous acts are those which it displeases you to do—and altruism is only enlightened self-interest—then an exaggerated quietism, a Yogi omphalos-stare, is the only good life; and then, where goes the state, whither flee manufactures, arts, manners, rational living, in fact all the impulses to civilization? In short, Mandeville was saying to the rigorists, 'Very well, let us take your assumptions and see where they lead. I, it goes without saying, agree with you that any action which has the least taint of self about it is vice; and if these things must be, for the good of all, do not let us at any time forget that they are vicious.' He is throughout ironical, he has his tongue in his cheek. 'I could never believe', Coleridge wrote, 'that Mandeville really meant anything more by his Fable of the Bees than a *bonne bouche* of solemn raillery.' That is true; but the gist of the raillery was 'Clear your minds of cant!' and never cease from examining into yourselves. Take it as such, and like many another piece of writing, thrown out, as this confessedly was, to divert the idle reader (the reader, that is, who liked speculation) and judged scandalous, it may well turn out to be a severe moral discipline. Jowett, who did not like the work, was of opinion that it was not 'a bad thing to read the book with patience and ask how much it is true of ourselves'.

The now somewhat formidable looking treatise on psychology, philosophy, sociology, economics, and a few minor points besides, first made its appearance as a trifling pamphlet of doggerel verse which was popular enough to be pirated. It read like an amusing squib directed against anybody whom you might happen to envy or dislike, or as an equally amusing justification of whatever kind of life you might care to lead. Nothing further appeared for some time, until indeed 1714, when a new edition came out, in company with 'An Enquiry into the Origin of Moral Virtue', and a number of Remarks, or essays explanatory of various parts of the poem, the whole being called *The Fable of the Bees: or Private Vices, Publick Benefits*. In the interval Mandeville had done some profound thinking, though he had found no cause to change any of his opinions; but in the Remarks he could elucidate and argue in prose what had before been stated in provocative, gnomic verse, which certainly called for a little elaboration. It would appear that he was impelled, even irritated to write, by the general trend of thought of his time. The 'Enquiry into Moral Virtue' goes to show that he pretended to adopt the ascetic, rigoristic attitude through unbelief in the rationalist scheme of things, in which it was largely assumed, even by Locke, that reason alone is required to light the path to virtue; and that the ways of nature, if rightly interpreted, lead men to act according to the will of God. The people who believed that, were the very people who at the same time 'give the name of Virtue to every performance, by which man, contrary to the impulse of nature, should endeavour the benefit of others, or the conquest of his own passions out of a rational ambition of being good'.

But you might, at any rate intellectually, as an entertaining game, accept the rigoristic standpoint. Far worse was the optimism expressed in the journals which adorned every tea-table:

When the incomparable Mr. Steele, in the usual elegancy of his easy style, dwells on the praises of his sublime species, and with all the embellishments of rhetoric sets forth the excellency of human nature, it is impossible not to be charmed with his happy turns of thought, and the politeness of his expressions. But though I have often been moved by the force of his eloquence, and ready to swallow the ingenious sophistry with pleasure, yet. . . .

and from that 'yet' was built a completely opposite philosophy. Addison, the 'silent parson in a tye-wig' as Mandeville called him, is not mentioned: but Addison had this at least in common with Mandeville—he believed in the necessity for hypocrisy, the difference being that Addison did not mind people deceiving themselves, whereas Mandeville objected very strongly. And there was Shaftesbury, who, however, does not seem so far to have taken such a hold on cultivated minds as to goad Mandeville to expostulation: that was to come later.

The *Fable* went into a second edition that same year, but it was not until 1723, when a new edition appeared, with the Remarks expanded, an attack on Charity Schools, and a 'Search into the Nature of Society', that the book attracted much attention. It was the sort of attention most people would have disliked, but it must have hugely tickled Mandeville. The Grand Jury of Middlesex presented the book as a public nuisance, and 'an abusive letter to Lord C.' enlivened the pages of the *London Journal*. The Grand Jury boomed splendidly: the *Fable* was 'a diabolical attempt against religion'; they conceived it was intended to 'debauch the nation'. The author of the 'Letter to Lord C.' regarded the work as 'so stunning, so shocking, so frightful, so flagrant an enormity', that it was likely the whole nation would become involved in the Divine Vengeance. Mandeville answered the accusations by pointing out that

the impugners of his moral standpoint simply had
not the wit to understand his book. Of a certain
attacked passage on the benefit of evil, he wrote:

I will likewise own very freely, that, if I had wrote with a
design to be understood by the meanest capacities, I would not
have chose the subject there treated of; or if I had, I would
have amplified and explained every period, talked and distinguished magisterially, and never appeared without the fescue
in my hand.

And later, rather more tartly: 'It is ridiculous for men
to meddle with books above their sphere.' The
defence in general is sound, except where the Charity
Schools are concerned; and in his way of thinking
even there it was sound, for he occupied a point of
view which few would wish to share with him. It is,
in effect, that for a nation to be prosperous, it must
have a large proportion of people so ignorant that
they will find it no hardship to perform the disagreeable, ill-paid labour so necessary to the state. Some
such proposition, very modified, is probably true;
but its statement at the extreme cannot but be re-
pugnant, and can only be defended by reiteration.

And again, Mandeville asked, do books really do
any harm—or good? 'If you ask me,' Mandeville had
said in his Preface, 'why I have done all this, *cui
bono*? and what good these notions will produce?
truly, besides the reader's diversion, I believe none
at all.' Mankind had remained the same in spite of
all the moralistic writings that had dotted the ages.
However, though a thing may be useless, at least it
can be susceptible of utility:

If I was asked, what naturally ought to be expected of 'em

[these notions], I would answer, that in the first place, the people, who continually find fault with others, by reading them would be taught to look at home, and examining their own consciences, be ashamed of always railing at what they are more or less guilty of themselves; and that in the next, those who are so fond of the ease and comforts, and reap all the benefits that are the consequence of a great and flourishing nation, would learn more particularly to submit to those inconveniences, which no government on earth can remedy, when they should see the impossibility of enjoying any great share of the first, without partaking likewise of the latter.

And if the book did no good, at least it diverted readers, for in the next few years it ran into several editions; and in 1732 Mandeville issued another volume, a second part, made up of six dialogues, in which 'these notions' are further expanded, and a disciple of Shaftesbury is neatly and with humour tangled in the Mandeville net.

For among 'free-thinkers', it was Shaftesbury who stood out as Mandeville's great rival, and he had already been attacked in the 'Search into the Origins of Society'. Shaftesbury was no more rigoristic than Mandeville, as we can see from so typical a passage of the *Characteristicks* as this:

So that in a sensible creature, that which is not done through any affection at all, makes neither good nor ill in the nature of that creature, who then is only supposed *good*, when the good or ill of the system to which he has relation is the immediate object of some passion or affection moving him.

Since it is therefore by affection merely that a creature is esteemed good or ill, natural or unnatural; our business will be to examine which are the good and natural, and which the ill and unnatural affections.

That was all very well, but what was this system?
Mandeville could see none. Besides, it was his
business, and his delight, to show that even the
'good' affections are only a form of egotism. But
how could there not be a natural antagonism between
the two minds?—between Mandeville, very *terre à
terre*, whose style, 'plebeian as it is,' Mr. Saintsbury
has written, 'may challenge comparison with the
most famous literary vernaculars in English for racy
individuality,' and Shaftesbury, elegant stoic, the
exponent of 'taste', always a trifle high-falutin', and
likely at any moment to fly off into the empyrean.
'His notions, I confess,' Mandeville wrote, 'are
generous and refined: they are a high compliment to
human-kind . . . What pity it is that they are not
true.' For he looked upon 'virtue and vice as per-
manent realities that must ever be the same in all
countries and in all ages'. Fiddlesticks!

And then, besides his infuriating softness, his
pomposity! In the first dialogue, Cleomenes (whom
we take to represent Mandeville) has occasion to
argue from a poor woman who had sold her son to be
a chimney sweep; upon which Horatio remarks, 'You
don't vie, I see, with Lord Shaftesbury for loftiness
of subjects'. Instead of taking a leaf out of Socrates'
book, Mandeville goes off in a comic enough parody:

When in a starry night with amazement we behold the
glory of the firmament, nothing is more obvious than that the
whole, the beautiful *All*, must be the workmanship of the
great Architect of power and wisdom stupendious; and it is
as evident, that every thing in the Universe is a constituent
part of one entire fabric.

Scratch an idealist, Mandeville seems to say, and you find a rhetorician.

But, it will be asked, seeing that we do in actual practice distinguish between virtue and vice; that there are some actions which are meritorious, which make for the good of all, and which we admire, how does it come that these actions occur although all men are vicious? Mandeville's answer is, that there are indeed these actions; but the 'virtues'—honour, chastity, generosity, self-restraint, modesty, and so on—are not virtues according to the rigoristic definition, but vices; for they are all founded upon passions, and the ruling passion (it was the age of ruling passions) is pride, the desire to be well thought of; upon conscience, which, he would agree with Dryden's phrase, was 'the foolish pride of doing well'. And indeed it is not so easy to get behind this doctrine; even Benjamin Franklin could not be so sure. He had added 'Humility', as an afterthought, to the table of virtues in which he was systematically to exercise himself, and was forced to admit of pride, that 'even if I could conceive that I had completely overcome it, I should probably be proud of my humility'. And Mandeville has no difficulty in showing that pride, the encouragement of the spirit of emulation, the stress laid on obtaining the approval of others, is the basis of all education, a claim to which Lord Chesterfield would not have made the slightest objection. And pride is a vice; passion enters into it. It is to be distinguished from self-love, which is the brute instinct of self-preservation, and is to be known, rather, as self-liking.

Further, a doctrine which raised as much ire as this of universal and beneficent vice was that of the necessity for luxury: and it was on this point mainly that Berkeley attacked Mandeville in his second *Alciphron* dialogue. But Berkeley, it must be confessed, though his style is inimitable, the working of his mind always delightful, his fun delicious, took somewhat too easy a way to destroy this particular 'minute philosopher'. Mandeville did not say that all vices were good, and ought to be encouraged, though he did suggest that all vices do produce a certain amount of good in the way of trade and the circulation of money. His argument was rather, as he pointed out in the *Letter to Dion* (Berkeley), that certain vices may by wise statesmanship be directed to the good of the state. The argument for luxury is, of course, within limits sound, so long as exports pay for imports, as Mandeville was careful to point out: it is known nowadays as the 'expansionist theory'. It was, to be sure, upheld by Dr. Johnson, who said that Mandeville 'opened his views into real life very much'. Yet it was he who made what is perhaps the soundest criticism of the *Fable*:

The fallacy of that book is, he remarked to Miss Seward, that Mandeville defines neither vices nor benefits. He reckons among vices every thing that gives pleasure. He takes the narrowest system of morality, monastic morality, which holds pleasure itself to be a vice, such as eating salt with our fish, because it makes it eat better; and he reckons wealth as a public benefit, which is by no means always true. . . . Mandeville puts the case of a man who gets drunk at an alehouse; and says it is a public benefit because so much money is got by it to the public. But it must be considered, that all the good gained by this, through the graduation of ale-house keeper, brewer, maltster, and farmer, is overbalanced by the evil caused to the man and his family by his getting drunk. . . . It may happen that good is caused by vice, but not as vice.

That, of course, is the point; Mandeville in his whole theory ignores the individual, and rates human happiness too low. What is the good, we may ask, of the most prosperous state, if no one can enjoy his pride? for that is the position we should reach if we were to push one side of Mandeville's argument as far as it will go. But then it is difficult to tell what his own view really was; that is the drawback of irony. It is a 'dangerous figure'.

This is not the place in which to rank Mandeville as a philosopher, to dovetail his system into that of his contemporaries and forebears; but it is interesting to note the effect he had. Apart from Pope, who could not resist a philosophy which gave such scope to a ruling passion, he has had little influence on 'pure' literature. But Adam Smith is based on Mandeville, not only for his economics, but also for his *Theory of the Moral Sentiments*; and, surprisingly, Rousseau is among his disciples. He is also the father of Utilitarianism, and Bentham, though he renounced some of his doctrine, may be said to derive largely from him. So far for influence. But what is most astonishing is the way in which, fumblingly no doubt, he anticipated some of the more modern conclusions, particularly in the realm of psychology. Much of what he says of shame,

clothing, and morality generally, may seem commonplace to us now; but it is only in the last thirty or
forty years that it has become so, thanks chiefly to
ethnologists. And we can go still further. As his
recent learned editor, Mr. F. B. Kaye, writes:

In other ways, also, Mandeville anticipated some of the
most recent developments of psychology. The fundamental
position of the *Fable*—that so-called good arises from a con-
version of so-called evil—is really a form of the chief tenets
of psycho-analysis—that virtues arise through the individual's
attempt to compensate for original weaknesses and vices.
Mandeville also forestalled another Freudian position when
he argued that the naturalness of a desire could be inferred
from the fact of a general prohibition aimed at it, and the
strength of the desire from the stringency of the prohibition.
And the psycho-analytical theory of the ambivalence of the
emotions was anticipated by Mandeville in his *Origin of
Honour*.

But where he would seem to rank highest, is as a
pioneer in the psychology of economics.

The main question for us, however, is not to discover his place in history, nor to judge of his influence, but to decide whether his writing can give us
delight at the present time; and indeed profit also,
for it does none of us any harm to be brought up
short in the pursuit of our virtues to inquire what
they really are. If the path of vice is a downhill one,
the path of virtue may well run in the same direction,
priggishess apart. The question, in fact, is much the
same as it was in Mandeville's day; we shall enjoy
the *Fable* if we like speculation, for the thought is
still fresh enough to make 'the cleverest, wickedest

book in the language' as Crabb Robinson called it,
a continual surprise. And, moreover, there is
Mandeville himself to know and like, his irony to
smile at. His butt, in the long run, is human inconsistency, the pretensions to virtue of all men in
nature. 'I say all men in Nature', Mandeville
explains, 'because devout Christians, who alone are
to be excepted here, being regenerated, and preter-
naturally assisted by the Divine Grace, cannot be
said to be in Nature.' That may be parson-baiting
but it is not an attack on Christianity; it is a dig at
humbug. It is doubtful, however, if Mandeville was
a Christian, although he loudly claimed to believe in
it, if usually as an impossible ideal. He was what we
should nowadays, using the term loosely, call a
rationalist; at all events a humanist. However sub-
versive of right behaviour his doctrine may appear,
his beliefs, if again we are right in our guesswork,
'had made no alteration in his conduct'. But then,
he confessed, he could not altogether wean himself
from pride, that basis of the social virtues. He un-
doubtedly lacked all sense of the transcendental;
certain emotions, such as the luxury of self-abasement,
were foreign to him; he knew nothing of the glory
to himself alone of a man's self-sacrifice. We
imagine him as tolerant, easy-going towards others,
ready to encourage compassion in himself, ready to
enjoy what money could bring him, but considering
no delight equal to that of self-examination, and the
tracing of motives in others. 'This elevation of mind
caused his chief pleasure', and whatever the rigorists
might demand of him, he would not sacrifice the

heart so far as to forego it. And though with Dr. Johnson we may condemn this book, as Mrs. Thrale said he did, we need have no hesitation in admitting with him, 'that it was the work of a thinking man'.